INTO  YOUR HANDS

Meditations and Prayers

INTO YOUR

on the Passion, Death, and

HANDS

Resurrection of Jesus Christ

EXCERPTS FROM
THE WRITINGS OF
SAINT ALPHONSUS LIGUORI

Edited by **NORMAN J. MUCKERMAN**, C.Ss.R.

Liguori
LIGUORI, MISSOURI

Imprimi Potest:
Richard Thibodeau, C.Ss.R.
Provincial, Denver Province
The Redemptorists

Published by Liguori Publications
Liguori, Missouri
www.liguori.org

Library of Congress Cataloging-in-Publication Data

Liguori, Alfonso Maria de', Saint, 1696–1787.
    Into your hands : meditations and prayers on the passion, death, and Resurrection of Jesus Christ / excerpts from Saint Alphonsus Liguori and F.X. Durrwell ; edited by Norman J. Muckerman.— 1st ed.
        p.   cm.
    ISBN-13: 978-0-7648–0789-3 ; ISBN-10: 0-7648-0789-7 (pbk.)
    1. Jesus Christ—Passion—Meditations. 2. Jesus Christ—Passion—Prayer-books and devotions—English. I. Durrwell, F.-X. (François-Xavier), 1912– II. Muckerman, Norman J. III. Title.

BT431 .L52 2001
232.96—dc21   2001038029

Printed in the United States of America
10 09 08 07 06   6 5 4 3 2

*For my confrere
and friend,
Father Gerry Resch, C.Ss.R.,
who has suffered more,
and with more patience,
than any person I know.*

NORMAN J. MUCKERMAN, C.Ss.R.

CONTENTS

FOREWORD BY THE EDITOR

The story in this book is true; in fact, it is a true love story. To be even more precise, it is the greatest true love story ever written!

This love story was written by Saint Alphonsus Maria de Liguori, Doctor of the Church, and founder of the Congregation of the Most Holy Redeemer, whose members are more commonly called the Redemptorists. This is one of the hundred or so books written by Saint Alphonsus during his long and productive life (1696–1787). He was born in Naples, and lived most of his life in southern Italy, where he is still well known and venerated.

This book contains a series of meditations (Alphonsus called them "Considerations") on the sad and agonizing events of the passion and death of Jesus. It is the last of three separate collections of meditations which Alphonsus wrote on this subject. The first series, written in 1759, was named *Reflections and Affections on the Passion of Jesus Christ.* In the sequel, which came out two years later, Alphonsus successfully merged the accounts given in the four gospels, entitling it *A Simple Exposition of the Circumstances of the Passion of Jesus Christ.* His third collection of "Considerations," which form the basis for this book, appeared in September 1773.

Alphonsus wrote this last collection of meditations primarily for his own use. He was by then seventy-seven years old and already preparing for his own death. Although he had previously written a book on this subject—entitled *Preparation for Death*—he felt that it was important for all Christians to read and recall something about the passion of Jesus every day. He often said that Jesus' passion was "for the saints a continual subject of meditation."

Curiously, this advertence to, or concentration on, the sufferings and death of Jesus is something unique to Christian spirituality. Other major world religions, such as Islamism or Buddhism, do not appear to admit to this kind of weakness in their founding prophets. Buddhists, however, do recognize the existence of suffering, but do not relate it to redemption, either their own or that of their neighbor. A believer merely accepts suffering as something he must experience along his path to "Nirvana." One of the basic beliefs of Islamism is that there cannot be any earthly manifestation of Allah (the Supreme Being); therefore the concept of redemption through a "Suffering Servant," who is God-made-man, is difficult to entertain.

To some degree, the Christian version of salvation history would also be difficult to entertain without Jesus' resurrection to complete it—and to give it the radiance of victory. However, only recently have Christian theologians linked Jesus' resurrection to the story of his passion and death. Perhaps it was for this reason that Alphonsus, despite his abiding faith in the redemption wrought by Jesus, concluded his meditations on the passion and death of Jesus with three short sections entitled "Meditations for the Easter Festival." However, these chapters treat the joys of heaven and the beatific vision rather than the meaning of the Resurrection.

Because of this, I have added a final chapter to this book. It is based on a work by a renowned theologian, a fellow Redemptorist, Father Francis X. Durrwell, C.Ss.R. This book, entitled *The Resurrection: A Biblical Study,* was published by Sheed and Ward in 1950. I hope our holy Father, Alphonsus Maria de Liguori, will not mind the intrusion.

NORMAN J. MUCKERMAN, C.SS.R.
MARCH 15, 2001
FEAST OF SAINT CLEMENT MARY HOFBAUER

INTRODUCTION

WHY MEDITATE ON THE SUFFERINGS AND DEATH OF JESUS?

Jesus, our Lord and Savior, declared that the reason he came to earth was to enkindle the fire of love in our hearts. "I came to bring fire to the earth, and how I wish it were already kindled!" (Lk 12:49).

And truly, what beautiful flames of love has Jesus ignited in so many human hearts, especially through the pain he chose to suffer while dying on the cross. He died such a horrible death in order to prove his unlimited love for us! Consequently, how many devout persons have become burning furnaces of love by meditating upon the wounds of Jesus! How many have consecrated their lives, their possessions, and their entire being to him through their love for a God who, even though he was divine, chose to become man and suffer so much out of love for them!

Those who meditate on the sufferings of Jesus follow the advice given in the Letter to the Hebrews: "Consider him who endured such hostility against himself from sinners, so that you may not grow weary or lose heart" (Heb 12:3). The great Saint

Augustine was mindful of this good advice when he prayed using these words: "Imprint, O Lord, your wounds in my heart, that I may read therein suffering and love: suffering, that I may endure all suffering for you; love, that I may despise all other loves but yours."

And from what other source did so many saints draw their courage and the strength to suffer torments, martyrdom, and death, if not from the very sufferings of the crucified Jesus? One such example is the compelling story of Saint Joseph of Leonessa, a Capuchin friar, who had to undergo painful surgery. The accepted medical practice of the time was to bind the patient's hands and legs to immobilize him for the operation. As the physicians began to bind him, Saint Joseph took hold of his crucifix and said: "Why these cords? Why these cords? Behold, here are my cords, my chains—my Savior nailed to the cross for me. Through his own sufferings, Jesus helps me to bear every trial for his sake." Thus, crucifix in hand, he suffered the amputation without complaint, looking upon Jesus who acted "like a lamb that is led to the slaughter, / and like a sheep that before its shearers is silent, / so he did not open his mouth" (Isa 53:7).

How can we complain about suffering we may deem to be undeserved when we see that Jesus was "wounded for our transgressions, / crushed for our iniquities" (Isa 53:5)? How can we refuse to obey when we learn that Jesus "humbled himself / and became obedient to the point of death— / even death on a cross" (Phil 2:8)? How can we seek to escape outrages and ignominies which may be justly or unjustly leveled against us when we behold Jesus who was treated as a fool, mocked as a false king, beaten, battered and spit upon, and finally, hung upon an evil cross on the hill of Calvary? In truth, when we see that he died as a result of the magnitude and multiplicity of sufferings and insults thrown at him in order to capture our hearts and our love, who could love anyone other than Jesus?

Saint Bonaventure wrote the following about frequent meditation on the passion and death of Jesus: "He who desires to go on advancing from virtue to virtue, from grace to grace, should meditate continually on the passion of Christ. There is no practice more profitable for the entire sanctification of the soul than this." And Saint Augustine said that a single tear shed at the remembrance of the passion of Jesus is worth more than a pilgrimage to Jerusalem, or a year fasting on bread and water.

Saint Paul is even more emphatic in what he wrote to the people of Corinth: "When I came to you, brothers and sisters, I did not come proclaiming the mystery of God to you in lofty words or wisdom. For I decided to know nothing among you except Jesus Christ, and him crucified" (1 Cor 2:1–2).

In fact, where can we better learn the science of the saints, that is, the science of loving God, than from Jesus crucified? One day, Saint Thomas Aquinas was visiting his friend Saint Bonaventure and asked him from which books he had drawn all the beautiful lessons in spirituality he had written. Bonaventure showed Thomas his crucifix, darkened and worn from the many kisses he had given it, and said: "This is my book. Everything I write comes from it. It has taught me whatever little I know."

One could truly say that the saints have learned the art of loving God from the study of the crucifix. Saint Francis of Assisi was one such saint. He wept so continuously while meditating on the great sufferings of Jesus that he almost lost his sight. One day, when he was seen weeping, someone asked if there was anything wrong. "What is wrong with me?" He replied, "I weep over the sorrows and insults offered to my Lord Jesus. I weep when I think of the many ungrateful people who do not love him, but live without any thought of him." Every time Francis heard a lamb bleating he was deeply affected by the thought of Jesus, the Lamb of God, dying on the cross for our sins. He constantly urged his brothers to be ever mindful of the passion of Jesus.

Primarily, this book on the sufferings, death, and resurrection of Jesus is meant to teach us to have a lively fear of sin. It also seeks to inflame us with love for a God who loved us so much that he suffered such a bitter death just to prove this love. Finally, it aims to give us the hope and confidence that, just as for Jesus, for us there is life after life. We are an Easter people, and Alleluia is our song!

Let us beseech Mary, the mother of Jesus and our Mother, to obtain for us from her son the graces we need to love a God who has loved us so much!

ALPHONSUS DE LIGUORI

JESUS:
THE SUFFERING SERVANT
(ISAIAH 52:13–15; 53:1–12)

See, my servant shall prosper;
he shall be exulted and lifted up,
and shall be very high.
Just as there were many who were
astonished at him
—so marred was his appearance,
beyond human semblance,
and his form beyond that of
mortals—
so he shall startle many nations;
kings shall shut their mouths
because of him;
for that which had not been told
them they shall see,
and that which they had not
heard they shall
contemplate.

*Who has believed what we have
        heard?
    And to whom has the arm of the
        Lord been revealed?
For he grew up before him like a
        young plant,
    and like a root out of dry ground;
he had no form or majesty that we
        should look at him,
    nothing in his appearance that
        we should desire him.
He was despised and rejected
        by others;
    a man of suffering and
        acquainted with infirmity;
and as one from whom others hide
        their faces
    he was despised, and we held
        him by no account.*

*Surely he has borne our infirmities
    and carried our diseases;
yet we accounted him stricken,
    struck down by God,
    and afflicted.
But he was wounded for our
        transgressions,
    crushed for our iniquities;
upon him was the punishment that
        made us whole,
    and by his bruises we are healed.*

All we like sheep have gone astray;
  we have all turned to our
    own way,
and the LORD *has laid on him*
  the iniquity of us all

He was oppressed, and he was
      afflicted,
  yet he did not open his mouth;
like a lamb that is led to the
      slaughter,
  and like a sheep that before its
      shearers is silent,
  so he did not open his mouth.
By a perversion of justice he was
      taken away.
  Who could have imagined his
      future?
For he was cut off from the land of
      the living,
  stricken for the transgression of
      my people.
They made his grave with the
      wicked
  and his tomb with the rich,
although he had done no violence,
  and there was no deceit in
      his mouth.

Yet it was the will of the LORD *to*
    crush him with pain.

*When you make his life an offering
    for sin,
   he shall see his offspring, and
      shall prolong his days;
through him the will of the LORD
      shall prosper.
   Out of his anguish he shall
      see light;
he shall find satisfaction through
      his knowledge.
The righteous one, my servant,
      shall make many righteous,
   and he shall bear their iniquities.
Therefore I will allot him a portion
      with the great,
   and he shall divide the spoil with
      the strong;
because he poured out himself
      to death,
   and was numbered with the
      transgressors;
yet he bore the sin of many,
   and made intercession for the
      transgressors.*

Chapter One

THE STORY OF THE PASSION: AN OVERVIEW

NECESSITY OF A REDEEMER AND PROPHECIES CONCERNING HIS COMING

When Adam, the first human being created by God, sinned by disobeying the Creator's command, his guilt was passed on to all his descendants. But since his offense was directed towards a God of infinite majesty, neither he, nor any of his descendants, would be able to offer an adequate apology or make worthy amends for the insult. Pardon for such an offense against the infinite God could only be requested by a divine person.

For this reason, the Son of God, the second Person of the Blessed Trinity, moved by compassion and filled with mercy for the human race, offered to take on human flesh and die for humankind. In this way, he would offer complete satisfaction to the Father for all our sins, and, for us, obtain the grace that was lost when Adam sinned.

We must also must remember that our loving Redeemer came

upon this earth not only to destroy sin and all its consequences, but also to lead us, by word and example, to a knowledge and observance of the will of his Father so that we might obtain eternal life. For this reason, he renounced all earthly honors and riches, choosing to live a life of humility, poverty, and pain, finally dying in torment and anguish on the cross.

Jesus' lifestyle was completely opposite to what was expected by the Jewish people. Their projected image of the promised Messiah was of someone who would come to earth to triumph over all his enemies by force. They expected him to conquer his enemies and make his followers rich and powerful. This, of course, was neither the kind of redeemer God had promised—nor the one foretold by the prophets.

This point was confirmed first of all on the night before his death when Jesus clarified his real role by telling Pontius Pilate: "My kingdom is not from this world" (Jn 18:36). Secondly, long before this declaration, the prophets of old had promised that the Messiah would not bring earthly and temporal blessings but rather the "abundance of salvation, wisdom, and knowledge" (Isa 33:6). In his own time, Jesus, again using the words of Isaiah, offered relief for the penitent, pardon for sinners, and liberty for those enslaved by the devil: "He has sent me to bring good news to the oppressed, to bind up the brokenhearted, to proclaim liberty to the captives, and release to the prisoners" (Isa 61:1).

Jesus had to choose one of two ways to redeem us. One way was to follow a path of power and glory, the other to tread the road of insult and pain. Since Jesus did not come to earth solely to deliver us from eternal death, but to incite us to love him and all our fellow human beings as well, he chose the latter. As we read in the Letter to the Hebrews, our life on earth is to be spent "looking to Jesus, the pioneer and perfecter of our faith, who for the sake of the joy that was set before him endured the cross" (Heb 12:2). In order that he might satisfy divine justice on our behalf and, at the same time, inflame us with holy love for him, Jesus was willing to endure the burden of our sins, so that by dying on the cross, he might obtain grace and eternal life for us. This is what Isaiah proclaimed when he wrote: "Surely he has borne our infirmities and carried our diseases" (Isa 53:4).

In the Old Testament, there are two explicit symbols for the role which Jesus was to assume in salvation history. The first is that of the scapegoat, the animal which was designated by the high priest to be condemned to bear the sins of all people. This goat was loaded with curses and driven into the desert to be subjected to God's wrathful destruction. It was in this context that Saint Paul wrote of Jesus: "For our sake he made him to be sin who knew no sin, so that in him we might become the righteousness of God" (2 Cor 5:21). This passage means that Jesus took upon himself the character of a sinner and endured the pains due to us for our sins, in order to make us just before the Father.

The second symbol, which refers to Jesus dying on the cross, is that of the brazen serpent set upon a pole. When the Israelites who had been bitten by deadly serpents looked upon the brazen serpent, they were healed. In the gospel, Jesus spoke of himself in this context: "And just as Moses lifted up the serpent in the wilderness, so must the Son of Man be lifted up, that whoever believes in him may have eternal life" (Jn 3:14–15).

Jesus' shameful and bitter death is foretold in the Book of Wisdom, where we read: "Let us see if his words are true, and let us test what will happen at the end of his life; for if the righteous man is God's child, he will help him, and will deliver him from the hand of his adversaries" (Wis 2:17–18). Although this passage may also apply to the death of every just person, many of the Fathers of the Church, such as Saint Jerome, Saint Cyprian, and others, state that it refers principally to the death of Jesus. It also bears a haunting resemblance to the words uttered by Jesus' enemies as they watched him dying on the cross: "He trusts in God; let God deliver him now, if he wants to; for he said, 'I am God's Son'" (Mt 27:43). These enemies had chosen the shameful death on the cross for Jesus so that his name might be forever infamous, or even forgotten, as Jeremiah had foretold: "Let us cut him off from the land of the living, so that his name will no longer be remembered!" (Jer 11:19).

Jesus accepted suffering in his life and in his death. He lived and died to pay the price for our sins. By accepting the role of a sinner, he also submitted to circumcision as an infant and, later on, he submitted to being "redeemed" for a price when he was presented in the Temple. This acceptance of the role of "sinner" is also the reason he allowed himself to receive the baptism of repentance in the desert from his cousin, John the Baptist.

In his passion and death, we find him suffering even more because of our sins. He was nailed to the cross to atone for our wicked wanderings. He was stripped of his garments to atone for our selfishness. He accepted the insults and jeers of the crowd to atone for our pride. He submitted to the executioners to atone for our craving for power. He bore the crown of thorns to atone for our evil thoughts. He drank the bitter gall to make up for our intemperance. And finally, he endured physical pains throughout his entire sacred body to atone for our sins of sensuality.

With tears of repentance, let us thank our heavenly Father for having given his innocent Son to death in order to deliver us from eternal death. As we are reminded in Saint Paul's Letter to the Romans: "He who did not withhold his own Son, but gave him up for all of us, will he not with him also give us everything else?" (Rom 8:32). This love is expressed even more emphatically in John 3:16: "For God so loved the world that he gave his only Son, so that everyone who believes in him may not perish but may have eternal life."

In a word, the passion, death, and resurrection of Jesus Christ is our salvation. Whatever blessing, whatever salvation, whatever hope we have, we have it all in Jesus and his merits. As Saint Peter, filled with the Holy Spirit, said to the rulers and the people of Jerusalem: "There is salvation in no one else, for there is no other name under heaven given among mortals by which we must be saved" (Acts 4:12).

The great truth is that the Church has always taught, and still teaches today, that it is only through Jesus, our Redeemer, that we can be saved. As we contemplate this truth, we must also reflect that it was through the paschal mystery, and through his sufferings, death, and resurrection that Jesus effected our redemption. "He humbled himself, and became obedient to the point of death—even death on a cross" (Phil 2:8).

There are other scriptural quotations to support this truth. For example, Saint Paul writes that when we receive holy Communion, we ought to remember the Lord's death: "For as often as you eat this bread and drink the cup, you proclaim the Lord's death until he comes" (1 Cor 11:26). Again, earlier in that same letter, the apostle Paul tells us: "For I decided to know nothing among you except Jesus Christ, and him crucified" (1 Cor 2:2).

The apostle Paul knew that Jesus had been born in a cave, and had lived for some thirty years in a poor home, working as a carpenter. He also knew that after his resurrection, he had ascended into heaven. Why, then, did he say that he would know nothing but Jesus crucified? Because he understood that the death suffered by Jesus on the cross was what most moved him to love and obey God, and to love his neighbor, which were the virtues most specially taught by Jesus from the throne of his cross. As Saint Augustine wrote: "The cross was not only the instrument of death to the sufferer [Jesus], but also the throne from which he taught."

Oh, devout reader, let us try to imitate the Spouse of the Canticles who said: "With great delight I sat in his shadow" (Song 2:3). Let us often, but especially on Fridays, sit in the shadow of the cross and rest there awhile, with tender affection, contemplating Jesus' sufferings and his love for us as he hung in agony on that bed of pain.

PRAYER

O my Redeemer, you have sacrificed your life upon the cross so that you might not see me perish, and I have repeatedly been willing to lose you, my infinite good, by losing your grace. But the sight of you on the cross, my Jesus, assures me that you will not drive me from your face if I repent for having offended you, and desire to love you. I do repent, my loving Savior, and I desire to love you with all my heart, and nevermore be separated from you.

Mary, my Mother, refuge of sinners, you who shared so much in the sufferings of your Son, pray to him to pardon me, and to give me the grace to love him forever.

Chapter Two

THE INTERIOR SUFFERINGS
OF JESUS

THE IGNOMINY, SHAME, AND HUMILIATIONS
WHICH JESUS ENDURED FOR US

Let us consider some of the unique and distinct sufferings which Jesus bore during his passion and death. Many of these events had been foretold ages before by various prophets, especially Isaiah. In chapter 53 of the Book of Isaiah, we come across descriptions and details so realistic it almost seems as if the prophet is a fifth evangelist! In fact, Saint Augustine is quoted as saying that Isaiah's word about Jesus' sufferings call for meditation and tears, rather than explanations from other writers.

Isaiah begins his prophecy with these words: "Who has believed what we have heard? And to whom has the arm of the LORD been revealed?" (Isa 53:1). This same lack of belief in the person of Jesus is noted later when the evangelist Saint John testifies: "Although he [Jesus] had performed so many signs in their presence, they did not believe in him. This was to fulfill the word spoken by the prophet Isaiah: 'Lord, who has believed our message, and to whom has the arm of the Lord been revealed?'" (Jn 12:37–38).

Isaiah prophesied that even though Jesus would work miracles, the Jewish people would not accept him as the Messiah. This non-acceptance was, as we have already said, because they imagined the true Messiah would come in majesty and glory, revealing his "arm," that is, his power. Furthermore, they believed that after triumphing over his enemies, this Messiah would shower his chosen people with riches and honors.

Even more than this, they believed their savior would be tall, strong, and mighty, like the cedars of Lebanon. But Isaiah tells us, "he grew up…like a young plant, and like a root out of dry ground; …nothing in his appearance that we should desire him; he had no form of majesty that we should look at him, nothing in his appearance that we should desire him. He was despised and rejected by others; a man of suffering and acquainted with infirmity; and as one from whom others hide their faces he was despised, and we held him of no account" (Isa 53:2–3).

The first man, Adam, in his pride disobeyed the commands of God, and as a result brought ruin on us all. But Jesus, as the second Adam, through his humility and acceptance of the Father's will, became our redeemer. He was content to be treated as the lowest and most abject of all people, a man reduced to the depths of humiliation. All this happened as Isaiah had predicted: "Surely he has borne our infirmities and carried our diseases; yet we accounted him stricken, struck down by God, and afflicted" (Isa 53:4).

This truth prompted Saint Bernard to cry out: "Oh, Jesus, you are the lowest and the highest! You are humble and at the same time full of majesty! You are the shame of men and the glory of angels! No one is more exalted than you, no one more ridiculed!" Then he added: "If the Lord Jesus who is higher than all things has made himself the lowest of all things, then every one of us should want others to be preferred to us, and fear to be preferred to others."

Isaiah continues: "He was wounded for our transgressions, crushed for our iniquities; upon him was the punishment that made us whole, and by his bruises we are healed" (Isa 53:5). The innocent Jesus, who had no personal contact with sin, took upon himself the miseries of human nature, which are the punishment for sin. He made our sins his own. Thus, he was burdened with all the blasphemies, sacrileges, thefts, and cruelties, all the abominable actions that human beings have committed, or ever will commit. Thus, although "he was wounded for our transgressions," nevertheless (as Saint Paul writes), he "redeemed us from the curse of the law by becoming a curse for us" (Gal 3:13).

Saint Thomas comments that both the internal and external pains which Jesus suffered exceeded all other pains which can be endured in this life. With regard to external pains, he endured torments in all his senses. First, his sense of touch, because his body was so torn from the scourging. Again, his sense of taste, when he was given gall and vinegar to drink. Also, his sense of hearing, when he heard the mockeries and blasphemies of his enemies who jeered him as he hung on the cross. Finally, his sense of sight suffered as well when he was forced to look down upon his holy mother who was standing in sorrow at the foot of the cross.

He also suffered in all the members of his body. His head

was covered with a crown of thorns, his hands and feet were riven by nails, his face was covered with spit and bruised by hundreds of blows, his entire body was ripped and torn apart by the scourging. He was, in short, wounded from head to foot, so bloodied and beaten that Pilate had hoped to save him from crucifixion by showing him to the people in such a pitiable state, saying: "Here is the man!" (Jn 19:5).

Truly, as the prophet said, "The LORD has laid on him the iniquity of us all" (Isa 53:6). And Jesus, compelled by love, of his own free will, offered himself to accomplish the Father's will. It was as Isaiah had predicted: "He was oppressed, and he was afflicted, yet he did not open his mouth; like a lamb that is led to the slaughter, and like a sheep that before its shearers is silent, so he did not open his mouth" (Isa 53:7).

Indeed, Jesus chose to offer satisfaction to the Father for our sins so that he might deliver us from eternal damnation. And let us note that he did this voluntarily, through his goodness and out of love for us. As he said: "I lay down my life.... No one takes it from me, but I lay it down of my own accord" (Jn 10:17–18).

It is also important to remember that Jesus' physical sufferings were most cruel. Saint Ambrose, in writing about them, says that in suffering, Jesus has followers, but no equals. Many saints have tried to imitate Jesus in this regard, but none has borne as much pain as our Redeemer. He truly suffered more than all the penitents, more even than all the martyrs. Saint Thomas says that Jesus, in his own passion and death, chose to undergo a depth of pain which would be sufficient to satisfy abundantly and completely all the sins of the entire human race. And Saint Bonaventure writes that he chose to suffer as much pain as if he had committed all our sins. Thus, the prophecy of Isaiah was fulfilled: "It was the will of the LORD to crush him with pain" (Isa 53:10).

THE INTERIOR SUFFERINGS OF JESUS

Up until now, we have spoken only of the physical pains Jesus endured. Who can ever explain or comprehend the inner pains he suffered, the pains of his soul, which were a thousand times more severe than his bodily torments?

Jesus' inner torments were so great that, in the garden of Gethsemane, they caused a bloody sweat to pour forth from his body, evoking this painful admission: "I am deeply grieved, even to death" (Mt 26:38). This sorrow, which afflicted Jesus in the garden, was with him during his entire life, for, from the very first moment of his existence he had always before him the very cause of his grief, namely our ingratitude for the love he would show us in his passion and death.

Even the angel that Saint Luke says came to comfort him at this moment (see Lk 22:43) was of no great help. Saint Venerable Bede says that the comfort of the angel, instead of alleviating Jesus' pains, in fact increased them by making him more sensitive to them. Let us note that it was after the angel came that the sweat of Jesus "became like great drops of blood falling down on the ground" (Lk 22:44).

At this point, according to Saint Bonaventure, the agony of Jesus reached its summit. This was when Jesus became so terrified that he prayed to the Father to be delivered from suffering and death: "My Father, if it is possible, let this cup pass from me." He prayed in these terms to show us the depth of his agony in enduring a death so cruel; yet even so, in order to fulfill the will of the Father, he immediately added the words: "Yet not what I want but what you want" (Mt 26:39). And Saint Mark tells us that he continued to pray using these terms of resignation to God's will: "And again he went away and prayed, saying the same words" (Mk 14:39).

Along with the prophecies of Isaiah, there were also other revelations about the passion and death of Jesus in the Old Testament. In the Book of Psalms, for example, the great King David also predicted other incidents that would happen to our suffering Savior. In Psalm 22, which is a plea for deliverance from suffering, we find this piteous appeal: "My God, my God, why have you forsaken me?" (Ps 22:1), which are the very words that came from the bruised lips of Jesus as he hung on the cross. And, as we prayerfully meditate upon this psalm, we discover that David predicted Jesus would be crucified, that his hands and feet be pierced with nails, that he would be stripped of his garments, that upon these garments his executioners would cast lots, and that his enemies would gather beneath the cross to mock and insult him as he hung between heaven and earth!

It is noteworthy to see that both Saint Matthew and Saint John recall these prophecies in their gospel accounts. It was important that they did so, since their testimony reinforces the fact that Jesus is indeed the Savior of the world, and through his sufferings, death, and resurrection, he has made it possible for all of us to be saved.

Thus, it is a consolation for us to read, in Psalm 85, verse 10: "Steadfast love and faithfulness will meet; righteousness and peace will kiss each other." This prediction came true when, because of the sufferings of Jesus, we gained peace with God.

At the same time, divine justice was more than abundantly satisfied by the death of the Redeemer.

We say "more than abundantly" because it was not necessary for Jesus to endure so many sufferings and so much pain in order to save us. One single drop of his blood, one single prayer on his part would have been enough to save the whole world. But Jesus did so much more in order to strengthen our hope and inflame our love. He did so much more so that another prediction of David would be fulfilled: "With the LORD there is steadfast love, and with him is great power to redeem. It is he who will redeem Israel from all its iniquities" (Ps 130:7–8). His is a "copious redemption" indeed.

PRAYER

Oh, my Jesus, my Savior and my God, your precious blood is my hope, for with the price of that blood, you have redeemed me from hell as often as I have deserved it. I know that by losing your grace, I have condemned myself to an eternity of despair, far from heaven and far from you. But I say it again, your blood is my hope, and now I seek your pardon and grace. By your grace I now have a great desire to love you above all things. I am sorry for all my sins, and I trust that you will pardon me in your goodness and love.

Oh Mary, Mother of God and my Mother, obtain for me the grace to remain faithful to your son and my Redeemer. Amen.

Chapter Three

THE PHYSICAL SUFFERINGS OF JESUS

JESUS IS SCOURGED, CROWNED WITH THORNS, AND CRUCIFIED

S aint Paul wrote the following about Jesus: he "emptied himself, taking the form of a slave" (Phil 2:7). Commenting on this text, Saint Bernard explained that Jesus not only assumed the role of a servant, but that of a slave, so that he might be beaten as slaves were beaten.

The scourging was the most cruel of all the tortures Jesus suffered. Actually, it shortened his life because it caused Jesus to lose a great quantity of blood, thus becoming the principal cause of his death. Jesus truly did sweat blood in the garden of Gethsemane. He lost more of his blood when he was crowned with thorns and again later, when he was nailed to the cross. But he shed most of his precious blood during the brutal beating he suffered at the hands of the Roman soldiers.

Jesus had even predicted this horrible phase of his passion. "For he [the Son of Man] will be handed over to the Gentiles;

15

and he will be mocked and insulted and spat upon. After they have flogged him, they will kill him" (Lk 18:32–33). It was revealed to Saint Bridget that Jesus was stripped of his garments and bound to a pillar, and then so cruelly beaten that his entire body was lacerated, and his ribs were laid bare. Truly, as Isaiah had prophesied: "He was wounded for our transgressions, crushed for our iniquities" (Isa 53:5).

At some point during his torture, Jesus was crowned with thorns. Saint Matthew tells us how this happened: "Then the soldiers…stripped him and put a scarlet robe on him, and after twisting some thorns into a crown, they put it on his head. They put a reed in his right hand and knelt before him and mocked him, saying, 'Hail, King of the Jews!'" (Mt 27:27–29).

Our Blessed Lady herself revealed to Saint Bridget that this crown of thorns covered her Son's entire head, and the thorns were driven in with such force that his sacred blood gushed forth from his forehead, streaming down his entire face, covering it completely.

JESUS LED TO THE CRUCIFIXION

Then it was time for Jesus to begin his last journey, the long and painful journey up the hill of Calvary. After Pilate condemned Jesus to death by crucifixion, the soldiers brought in the cross. Jesus did not refuse it; he took the cross upon his shoulders. Saint Augustine calls this a "great mystery"; by this he means it is a great sign for those who would choose to follow Jesus. For the cross is the true standard under which these followers must be enrolled, the banner under which they must contend in order to become his companions in the kingdom of heaven.

There is a passage of Isaiah which reads: "For a child has been born for us, a son is given to us; authority rests upon his shoulders" (Isa 9:6). Commenting on these words, Saint Basil says that earthly rulers often load their subjects with unjust burdens to increase their own power. But Jesus chose to take upon himself the burden of the cross and carry it in order to give us life and through it, salvation. He also said that earthly kings often put their trust in the force of arms and in accumulating worldly riches; but Jesus found his power in the cross, by humbling himself and suffering, accepting the cross so that he might provide us with an example and the courage to follow him. That is exactly why he had earlier said: "If any want to become my followers, let them deny themselves and take up their cross and follow me" (Mt 16:24).

Writing about the cross, Saint John Chrysostom has strung together a beautiful series of expressions. He describes the cross, the instrument of Jesus' death, in the following terms:

- "The hope of Christians, especially those who are in despair." Would Christians, especially sinners, have any hope at all if Jesus had not died on the cross?
- "The guide for those at sea." We live our life traversing, as it were, a dangerous sea. The humiliation of the cross gives us the grace to keep God's laws, or to amend our lives if we have fallen into sin. As the Psalmist wrote: "It is good for me that I was humbled, so that I might learn your statutes" (Ps 119:71).
- "The counselor of the just." Good people learn wisdom in adversity; thus they are even more motivated by the cross to unite themselves closer to God.

- "Rest for the troubled." Where can those in distress find relief if not by looking to the cross upon which their Redeemer and God died in pain out of love of them?
- "The glory of the martyrs." The glory of the martyrs consists of the fact that they were able to unite their deaths to the painful death of Jesus on the cross. As Saint Paul said: "May I never boast of anything except the cross of our Lord Jesus Christ, by which the world has been crucified to me, and I to the world" (Gal 6:14).
- "The physician for those who are ill." The cross is a great remedy for those who are sick in spirit. Trials and tribulations help them to repent; they also separate them from worldly attractions.
- "The fountain for the thirsty." Those who are "thirsting" for holiness find Jesus through suffering. Saint Teresa used to say: "Oh, that I might suffer! Oh, that I might die!" Saint Mary Magdalene of Pazzi went even further. She said: "To suffer, and not to die," meaning that she was willing not to die, not to rejoice in heaven, in order to continue to suffer here on earth.

To tell the truth, everyone, whether good or bad, has a cross to carry. Good people, even though they enjoy peace of mind and a clear conscience, still have their troubles, their crosses. Sometimes God, in his goodness, comforts them; at other times, they are afflicted with bodily pains and infirmities, or suffer spiritual desolation, trials, scruples, temptations, and fears.

Sinners, for their part, carry much heavier crosses: remorse for their sins, the dread of eternal damnation, even pains and problems when things go wrong. When afflictions and adversities happen to good people, they can unite themselves to the divine will, and suffer in patience. But how can sinners remain calm or accept God's will when they remember that they are living in enmity with God? Thus, their pains and suffering continue without relief.

That added suffering given to sinners is the reason Saint Teresa used to say: "People who love God embrace the cross and thus do not feel its weight; those who do not love God drag it behind them, and thus cannot help but see it as a very heavy burden."

THE CRUCIFIXION OF JESUS

Saint Luke states it simply: "When they came to the place that is called The Skull, they crucified Jesus there with the criminals, one on his right and one on his left" (Lk 23:33). It was revealed to Saint Bridget that the executioners first nailed Jesus' right hand to the wood of the cross, then his left, and then his sacred feet. The cross was raised and fixed into the ground, and Jesus was left to die upon this bed of anguish.

This punishment of death on the cross was, says Saint Augustine, a most bitter torment because it was deliberately prolonged so that the criminal would feel the pain for a longer period of time. Imagine the horror in heaven at the sight of the Son of the Eternal Father crucified between two thieves! Another prophecy of Isaiah was truly fulfilled here: "He...was numbered with the transgressors; yet he bore the sin of many, and made intercession for the transgressors" (Isa 53:12).

Upon contemplating Jesus hanging on the cross, Saint John Chrysostom cried out in amazement and love: "I see Jesus always in the middle, in the middle of the Most Holy Trinity, in the middle on Mount Tabor between two saints, Moses and Elijah, and now in the middle on Calvary between two criminals." This last statement could come to pass only because of the divine decree that Jesus was to die bearing the sins of many, just as Isaiah foretold.

Again, looking to the book of Isaiah, we find the prophet asking an unusual question: "Why are your robes red, and your garments like theirs who tread the wine press?" (Isa 63:2). The prophet provides the answer: "I have trodden the wine press alone, and from the peoples no one was with me" (Isa 63:3). Several of the early Fathers of the Church, including Saint Augustine, explain that the wine press signifies Jesus' passion, during which his garments—that is, his holy human flesh—were sprinkled with blood. There is even a cryptic reference to this in the Book of Revelation: "He is clothed in a robe dipped in blood, and his name is called The Word of God" (Rev 19:13).

Behold, devout reader, your Lord and Savior, "the most handsome of men" (Ps 45:2), as he hangs on Calvary's cross, his body so disfigured by cruel punishments and torments that it struck horror in all who beheld it. Yet his deformities make him seem more beautiful in the eyes of those who love him, because his wounds, the residual marks of the flagellation, his torn and tattered flesh, are all signs and proof of his love for them. Saint Augustine goes so far as to say that his infirmities are our beauty, because through them, our own sinfulness and imperfections are cleansed and made whole. Again, as we read in the Book of Revelation: "These are they who have come out of the great ordeal; they have washed their robes and made them white in the blood of the Lamb" (Rev 7:14).

With the exception of the Blessed Virgin Mary, every person, even including the saints, was at one time tainted by sin, covered as it were with a defiled or soiled garment. But after they were washed with the blood of the Lamb, they became clean and agreeable to God.

JESUS HANGING UPON THE CROSS

When we look at Jesus hanging on the cross, we are totally amazed by this unbelievable mystery. It is a spectacle that fills heaven and earth with awe and wonder. First of all, it is a spectacle of justice in which the Eternal Father, in order to satisfy divine justice, punishes the sins of humankind represented by the person of his only-begotten Son, whom he loves as much as he loves himself. It is also a spectacle of mercy, in which this only Son dies a shameful and bitter death in order to save creatures from the punishment due them. But most of all, it is a spectacle of love, featuring a God who offered up his life to redeem his own enemies from death.

It is no wonder that this mystery has become, and ever will be, the most cherished object of contemplation for the saints and all earnest people. These are the people who, when they see the cross, not only wish to strip themselves of earthly pleasures and goods, but also joyfully embrace all pains and even death, so that they might show some gratitude to the God who died because of his love for them.

At the sight of Jesus dying on his cross, the saints have accepted mockery and contempt more than worldly people have sought the honors of the world. At the sight of Jesus on the cross with his sacred blood flowing from his many wounds, they have learned to abhor sensual pleasures and practice penance and self-denial. At the sight of the obedient Jesus hanging on the cross, they have sacrificed their own will and embraced a life of obedience. At the sight of the patient Jesus, willing to suffer so many pains and insults for our love, they have received with satisfaction and even joy injuries and persecution at the hands of others, as well as sicknesses, sufferings, and other common infirmities of living. Finally, at the sight of Jesus on the cross offering himself over to the Father in the supreme sacrifice, they have also given to God everything they possessed— property, pleasures, honors, even life itself.

PRAYER

O my crucified Jesus, to make yourself loved by us you have spared nothing. You have even given up your life to die a most painful death. How then can I, who love my relatives, my friends, and even animals from whom I receive only small tokens of affection, how can I be so ungrateful as to despise your grace and your love, for the sake of petty pleasures and vain delights! For things of no worth, I have turned my back to you. I deserve to be banished by you as I have so often banished you from my life. But I know that you continue to ask me to love you: "You shall love the Lord your God!" So then, my Jesus, as you desire that I should love you, and offer me pardon for my sins, I declare that I renounce my sins and wish to turn back to you. Henceforth I wish only to love you, my Savior, my Creator, my Redeemer, my Love.

Mary, my Mother, refuge of sinners, pray for me and obtain for me the grace of loving God. I ask for nothing more. Amen.

Chapter Four

THE INSULTS JESUS ENDURED
WHILE ON THE CROSS

"IF YOU ARE THE SON OF GOD, COME
DOWN FROM THE CROSS"

U ntil now, we have primarily considered the dreadful
physical pains which Jesus suffered from the time of his
arrest in Gethsemane up to his crucifixion on Calvary. We have
seen him as he "endured the cross, disregarding its shame" (Heb
12:2). We have observed him being nailed to that infamous bed
of pain. We have beheld him hanging there for three long hours,
unable to move, unable to obtain even the slightest alleviation
from the terrible sufferings that assaulted his entire body. It may
truly be said that while he was on the cross, he went through as
many deaths as the moments he spent on that gibbet of shame.

Yet it is even more true to say that while his physical, exte-
rior pains were unspeakably bitter, his interior, spiritual sufferings were even greater. His blessed soul was totally desolate
and deprived of all consolations. Within his loving heart, Jesus
felt consummate weariness and sorrow. It was this state of soul

that caused him to utter the heart-breaking cry: "My God, my God, why have you forsaken me?" (Mt 27:46).

Saint Matthew describes the circumstances that led up to this cry of apparent despair. A great number of people were milling about beneath the cross: scribes, elders, priests, soldiers, all of them adding to his suffering with their own form of insults and mockery. As the evangelist writes: "Those who passed by derided him, shaking their heads" (Mt 27:39). This was, in part, another aspect in fulfillment of David's prophecy: "All who see me mock at me; they make mouths at me, they shake their heads; 'Commit your cause to the LORD; let him deliver—let him rescue the one in whom he delights!'" (Ps 22:7–8).

Then, as Saint Matthew writes, they continued their cries of derision: "You who would destroy the temple and build it in three days, save yourself! If you are the Son of God, come down from the cross" (Mt 27:40). Note that Jesus had not said he wanted to destroy their temple. In fact, as we read in the famous story of Jesus cleansing the temple, when they demanded of him some sign that he had the authority and power to do what he did, Jesus had said: "Destroy this temple [referring to his own body], and in three days I will raise it up" (Jn 2:19). He was, of course, speaking allegorically at that time, foretelling his own resurrection.

"Save yourself," they said to him. How ridiculous was their suggestion! If Jesus, the Son of God who became man to save us, had wanted to save himself, he would not have voluntarily chosen death. "Come down from the cross," they urged him. But that would have defeated his whole purpose in becoming one of us; he would not have been able to accomplish our redemption and we would not have been delivered from eternal death. As Saint Ambrose writes: "He willed not to come down, lest if he did so, I myself would die."

Another spiritual writer suggests that Jesus' enemies hurled this particular challenge at the instigation of the devil, who was trying to prevent or hinder God's plan for our salvation. Saint John Chrysostom expresses yet another opinion saying that Jesus' enemies challenged him so that, if he should in fact really die on the cross, they would be able to say he was an impostor, regardless of the outcome, because while claiming to be the Son of God he was unable to save himself from death. This reason, adds the saint, is why Jesus did not come down from the cross until he was dead and had fulfilled his stated purpose in life: to save us by his death on the cross.

It was for this reason as well that Saint Paul wrote: "Christ redeemed us from the curse of the law by becoming a curse for us—for it is written, 'Cursed is everyone who hangs on a tree'—in order that in Christ Jesus the blessing of Abraham might come to the Gentiles" (Gal 3:13–14).

"HE SAVED OTHERS, HE CANNOT SAVE HIMSELF"

Jesus' enemies continued their insults while he hung on the cross. They scoffed at him even as the moment of his death approached. In their hatred, they recalled some of his miracles, especially those he worked to restore life to the dead. Look at him, they jeered, he saved other people, but now this impostor cannot even save his own life!

Saint Leo, responding to this insane charge, wrote that this was not the appropriate time for Jesus to display his divine power;

furthermore, he was not about to forestall the salvation of the human race just to dispute the blasphemies of his enemies. Saint Gregory suggested yet another reason why Jesus did not to come down from the cross. "If he had come down," he says, "he would not have shown us the virtue of patience." Jesus refrained from a demonstration of divine power and remained on the cross in order to teach us to have patience in times of suffering and pain, and to show us restraint, especially when other people try to harm us.

This example was followed by the saints who, when they were offended or persecuted, did not seek revenge. In fact, it was at times such as these they felt at ease and even rejoiced that they were called to bear insults for the sake of their faith.

"LET GOD DELIVER HIM NOW, IF HE WANTS TO"

This particular insult, carrying, as it does, more than a taint of blasphemy, refers directly to God the Father. It also, in a way, echoes a passage from the Book of Wisdom. There, we read these words: "The righteous man...professes to have knowledge of God, and calls himself a child of the Lord.... Let us see if his words are true, and let us test what will happen at the end of his life; for if the righteous man is God's child, he will help him, and will deliver him from the hand of his adversaries.... Let us condemn him to a shameful death, for, according to what he says, he will be protected" (Wis 2:12–13; 17–20).

We have already noted that from the manner in which they insulted Jesus, it is clear the chief priests were filled with envy and hatred for him. Yet it is also clear that they still feared this man who had performed so many miracles while claiming to be the Son of God. Now they wanted to make sure that he would die; they wanted to be present at his death, and, at the same time, be freed from any fear of punishment for having killed him. For this reason, as they saw Jesus growing weaker and coming closer to the end, they became more daring. And so they taunted him for his inability to save himself and also for the fact that, even though he claimed to be the Son of God, he had apparently been abandoned by the Father.

They were entirely in error, of course, for the Father truly loved Jesus, loving him all the more because of what he was voluntarily doing for our salvation. Jesus had stated this when he described himself as the good shepherd: "I lay down my life for the sheep…. For this reason the Father loves me, because I lay down my life in order to take it up again" (Jn 10:15, 17). The Father had already destined him to be the victim of the great sacrifice which would bring infinite glory to the Father and, at the same time, ensure the salvation of the entire human race. If the Father were to deliver Jesus from death, none of this could have happened.

There is also a special lesson here for us to learn. The insults hurled at Jesus as he was dying on the cross serve to remind us that, as his disciples, we must try to avoid anger and resentment when we are ridiculed or despised by others. Let us also not refuse to pardon those who might offend us, for when we pardon them, we will be imitating our humble Savior.

PRAYER

O my Jesus, how can I be disturbed by any insults I may receive from others, I who because of my sins have so often deserved the punishments of hell. By the merits of all the insults which you suffered while you were dying on the cross for me, give me the grace to suffer with patience any and all offenses against me. I love you above all things, and I desire to suffer for you who have suffered so greatly for me. I hope for every grace from you, who have redeemed me with your own blood. And I also hope for your intercession, my dear Mother Mary. Amen.

Chapter Five

THE SEVEN WORDS SPOKEN BY JESUS FROM THE CROSS

Editor's note: According to the gospels, Jesus made seven significant statements (referred to as *Words*) while dying on the cross. Throughout the years, each of these statements has been the subject of private meditations. They have also formed the basis for sermons given during the *Tre Ore* (three hours) devotions which were offered in Catholic churches on Good Friday afternoons, from noon until three o'clock. This chapter contains some of the comments Saint Alphonsus made about them.

THE FIRST WORD

*"Father, forgive them; for they do not know
what they are doing"*
(Lk 23:34).

See the love Jesus has even for his executioners! Saint Augustine writes that although they were involved in the process of nailing him to the cross, Jesus asks the Father to pardon them. He was thinking not so much about the brutal punishment they were inflicting upon him, but about the love he bore them.

Some may say: why did Jesus pray to the Father for their forgiveness when he could have pardoned them? Saint Bernard replies that he asked the Father, not because he was unable to forgive them, but so that he might teach us to pardon those who persecute us. "What a wonderful act," says the saint; "They cry: Crucify him! and he cries: Forgive!" Saint Augustine adds: Look at your God upon the cross; see how he prays for those who have crucified him, and then try to deny pardon to your brothers and sisters who have offended you!

Saint Leo says that this prayer of Christ on the cross was the reason that many thousands of residents of Jerusalem later came to believe in Jesus when the apostles preached to them on the first Pentecost.

PRAYER

O eternal Father, hear the prayer of your beloved Son who prayed to you to pardon us. We do not deserve this pardon, but Jesus has merited it. By his death he has more than abundantly satisfied for our sins. And now I repent, heavenly Father, with all my heart for having offended you, as I recall with confidence what Jesus has said of himself: "For the Son of Man has come to save the lost" (Mt 18:11).

THE SECOND WORD

"Truly I tell you, today you will be with me in Paradise"
(Lk 23:43).

In the gospel, Saint Luke tells how one of the two thieves who were crucified with Jesus remained hardhearted, while the other was converted. The obstinate thief even derided Jesus, saying:

"Are you not the Messiah? Save yourself and us!" (Lk 23:39). But the other thief, whom we now call Saint Dismas, rebuked his companion and then turned to Jesus, saying: "Jesus, remember me when you come into your kingdom" (Lk 23:42). Jesus then promised that he would be in paradise that very day: "Truly I tell you, today you will be with me in Paradise" (Lk 23:43).

Arnold of Chartres notes the virtues which the good thief practiced on this occasion: "He believed, he repented, he confessed, he preached, he loved, he trusted, he prayed."

How true this is. For through a wonderful act of grace, the good thief came to believe that Jesus, even though he was hanging on a cross of shame at the time, was about to enter into a glorious kingdom. He believed, says Saint Gregory, that the one he saw dying was about to reign.

He also repented. He confessed his sins openly: "And we indeed have been condemned justly, for we are getting what we deserve for our deeds" (Lk 23:41). Saint Augustine notes that the good thief did not have the courage to hope for pardon until he had confessed his guilt. Only then could he ask Jesus to remember him and take him into his kingdom. This is the reason that Saint Athanasius called him a blessed thief for he "stole a kingdom by his confession."

He also "preached" by declaring Jesus innocent: "But this man has done nothing wrong" (Lk 23:41b). And he also showed his love for God by accepting death with resignation, as a punishment for his sinful past: "We are getting what we deserve for our sins" (Lk 23:41a).

For these and other reasons as well, Saint Cyprian, Saint Jerome, and Saint Augustine all call this blessed thief a true martyr. He is called a martyr because, as tradition tells us, after he called Jesus innocent, the executioners broke his legs and generally treated him with added fury, but he accepted this further punishment most willingly.

This story of the good thief also provides us with other lessons about the goodness of God who always grants us more than we ask. Saint Ambrose says that the good thief asked only that Jesus remember him; but Jesus goes far beyond that, he promises the good thief that he would be in paradise that very day! Furthermore, as Saint John Chrysostom remarks, no one had merited paradise before this thief. This confirms what God promised through the prophet Ezekiel, namely, that when a sinner repents of his sins, God pardons him in the same way as if he had forgotten all of the sins the sinner committed: "But if the wicked turn away from all their sins that they have committed and keep all my statutes and do what is lawful and right, they shall surely live; they shall not die. None of the transgressions that they have committed shall be remembered against them" (Ezek 18:21, 22). God, says Saint Augustine, is always ready to embrace penitent sinners.

Thus, for the unrepentant thief, the cross became a precipice leading straight to hell, while for the good thief, it became a ladder to paradise.

PRAYER

O my Jesus, from now on I wish to sacrifice my life to you, and I hope that when I come to die, I will have the grace to unite my death to the sacrifice which you yourself offered on the cross. I hope to die in your grace, stripped of all earthly affections, and thus be able to love you with all my power throughout all eternity. Amen.

THE THIRD WORD

"Woman, here is your son.... Here is your mother"
(Jn 19:26, 27).

In the Gospel according to Saint John, we read: "When Jesus saw his mother and the disciple whom he loved standing beside her, he said to his mother, 'Woman, here is your son.' Then he said to the disciple, 'Here is your mother'" (Jn 19:26–27).

Saint Mark, in his gospel, tells us that, at the time of Jesus' crucifixion, many women were there, watching the sad spectacle from a safe distance. However, Saint John remarks that Mary, the Mother of Jesus, along with Mary Magdalene and Mary of Cleophas, were there as well, standing not far off, but close to the cross, actually beneath it, so that they might be near Jesus in his last agony.

One author of the life of Jesus describes the scene this way: "There were his friends who watched from afar; but the holy Virgin, the Magdalene, and the other Mary stood close to the cross, with John. Wherefore Jesus, seeing his mother and John, spoke to them directly." Truly, Mary was a mother who would not desert her son, even in the face of death. Other mothers might go away when they see their child dying; they cannot stand by, powerless, in that dreaded moment. But not Mary; the nearer her son approached death, the closer she drew to his cross.

Mary stood beneath the cross, and as Jesus was sacrificing his life for the salvation of the human race, she likewise offered her sufferings for the same cause, with perfect resignation sharing all the pains and insults which Jesus suffered. Those who describe Mary as fainting at the foot of the cross dishonor her courage and strength. She was a valiant woman, which is why Saint Ambrose wrote the following about her during this time of extreme distress: "I read of her standing there, but not of her weeping."

Mary's grief was great, but it was not barren, like the grief of other mothers who see their children suffer, but are generally unable to do much about it. Mary's grief was productive and fruitful, inasmuch as through it, and through her great love, she, who was the mother of the Savior, now became the mother of those who were saved as well. She, who was the natural mother of the head, now became the spiritual mother of the members, cooperating with him through her love by causing them to be born as children of the Church.

This, we believe, is the basic meaning behind the words Jesus spoke from the cross to Mary and Saint John. Obviously, the message has other implications, some of which we will discuss here.

For example, some persons might ask: if there were other persons present beneath the cross, why did Jesus only see Mary and John, and talk only to them? Saint John Chrysostom replies that love always makes us look more closely at the object of our love. Saint Ambrose says the same thing, specifically that it is only natural for us to see those we love most before any others.

Again, some may ask: why did Jesus call Mary "woman" and not "mother"? I answer that he called her "woman" because, now nearing death, he spoke as one about to depart this world to a person who would no longer have a son on earth. And so he gave her John, who would serve and love her as a son. We might also note that the words Jesus spoke would indicate that Saint Joseph was already dead at this point in time, for, if he were still alive, he would naturally have been present with his wife.

There was a further reason for Jesus to address Mary as "woman." This was to connect Mary with the great woman spoken about and foretold in the first pages of the Old Testament when God spoke to the serpent in the Book of Genesis: "I will put enmity between you and the woman, and between your off-spring and hers; he will strike your head, and you will strike his heel" (Gen 3:15).

No one will have any doubt that the woman spoken about and foretold in Genesis was the Blessed Virgin Mary, who, by means of her son, would crush the head of Satan. Or, perhaps it would be more correct to say that her son, by means of the woman who would give him birth, would accomplish this.

Nevertheless, Lucifer was the natural enemy of Mary: whereas he was proud, ungrateful, and disobedient, Mary was humble, grateful, and obedient.

It is as God said: "I will put enmity between you and the woman." This indicates that after Adam's fall, despite what the Son of God did to redeem the human race, there would still be two families, two blood lines in the world: the seed of Satan—the family of sinners; and the seed of Mary—the family of the just, with Jesus as the head. This is another reason we proclaim Mary as mother, both of the head and of the members, the faithful children of God.

PRAYER

O Mary, my suffering Mother, you and I know that I have deserved hell, and that I have no hope of salvation except by sharing in the merits of the death of your son, Jesus. Pray for me that I might obtain this precious grace. May I gain it through your intercession, you who saw your son, my Redeemer, bow his head on Calvary and die before your very eyes for my sake.

Therefore, O Queen of martyrs, advocate of sinners, help me always, and especially at the hour of my death. Obtain for me the grace of great confidence in Jesus as well as the grace of final perseverance. Jesus and Mary, I recommend myself to you! Amen.

THE FOURTH WORD

"My God, my God, why have you forsaken me?"
(Mt 27:46).

Saint Matthew writes that Jesus uttered these words "in a loud voice." Why, you might ask. One holy writer says that he cried out with such force to show his own divine power. Although he was near death, he was still able to cry out loudly, something ordinarily impossible for a dying person.

Saint Leo also tells us that Jesus' cry was not so much a complaint, as it was a lesson, since Jesus wished to use it to teach us how intensely evil sin is—for sin had compelled the Father to abandon his beloved Son without help or reassurance, only because he had taken the burden of our sins upon himself.

Although Jesus was not really abandoned by his Father at that time, nor was he deprived of the divine glory he had enjoyed since his coming on earth, he did not have the sense of comfort and relief that God ordinarily gives to his faithful servants during their sufferings. On the contrary, he was left in darkness, fear, and distress, in the kind of misery sinners deserve. Truly, he had already experienced a kind of desolation in the garden of Gethsemane; but what he suffered on the cross was far greater and more bitter.

In fact, the abandonment felt by Jesus on the cross was the most dreadful of all his sufferings. He accepted all the other torments without complaint; but the abandonment by his Father was too much. He cried out loudly, in deep grief, with many tears and prayers, as Saint Paul tells us. It was as though he sought to teach us how much he suffered in order to obtain God's mercy for us. It was as though he wanted us to understand how dreadful it is for sinners to be excluded from God's presence, and deprived of God's love. It seemed as if he wanted us to remember the words of the prophet Hosea: "I will drive them out of my house. I will love them no more" (Hos 9:15).

Commenting on Jesus' cry from the cross, Saint Augustine offers us a very comforting observation. He states that Jesus was indeed agitated at the sight of his death, but this agitation was for our comfort, should we find ourselves in a similar state. If we do, says the saint, we should not consider ourselves reprobates, or abandon ourselves to despair, but rather remember that even Jesus was disturbed at the sight of death.

If indeed we should become desolate of spirit, or deprived of a sense of the divine presence, let us unite our desolation to that which Jesus suffered on the cross. Let us make the same acts of conformity to God's will as Jesus did in the garden of Gethsemane, remembering that, as Saint Francis de Sales teaches, our God is as worthy of love when he hides himself as when he makes himself seen.

PRAYER

O my Jesus, through the merits of your own lonely death, do not deprive me of your help in that great struggle which I will have to undergo with the powers of evil in the hour of my own death. At that terrible hour all things of earth will have deserted me, or will no longer be of any help to me. But do not abandon me, you who have died for me and can alone come to my aid as I pass into eternity.

And you, Mary my Mother, pray for me now and at the hour of my death. Amen.

THE FIFTH WORD

"I am thirsty"
(Jn 19:28).

Saint John gives the background to Jesus' pain-filled statement: "After this, when Jesus knew that all was now finished, he said (in order to fulfill the scripture), 'I am thirsty.' A jar full of sour wine was standing there. So they put a sponge full of the wine on a branch of hyssop and held it to his mouth" (Jn 19:28–29).

In the Book of Psalms, David had already prophesied that this would happen: "And for my thirst they gave me vinegar to drink" (Ps 69:21). The bodily thirst which Jesus endured on the cross was most severe. He had already lost a great deal of blood: first in the garden of Gethsemane, then in the hall of judgment where he was scourged and crowned with thorns, finally, during the hours while he was hanging upon the cross, his sacred blood was gushing forth from his wounds. No wonder he suffered physical thirst!

But, as Blosius says, even more terrible was his spiritual thirst. This was the deep desire he had to save us and suffer more on our behalf in order to prove his love. As Saint Laurence Justinian writes: "This thirst came from the fount of love."

One sacred writer remarks on how interesting it is that Jesus makes no mention of any of the terrible pains he suffered during his crucifixion other than thirst. "Lord," he asks, "what are you thirsting for? You are silent about the cross, yet you cry out about your thirst?" Saint Augustine answers for Jesus, saying: "My thirst is for your salvation." Saint Basil adds that Jesus, by proclaiming his thirst, wants us to understand that he was dying with the desire to endure even more suffering than he had already undergone, so that we might learn to accept suffering for his sake.

PRAYER

O my Jesus, you have thus desired to suffer for me, and I become so impatient when I am asked to suffer even the slightest pain in my life here on earth. Sometimes I become unsupportable to others and even to myself. Through the merits of your patience during your own passion and death, help me to accept the crosses which come into my life. Make me more like you before I die.

Mary, my sorrowful Mother, give me a share of your tender heart. Amen.

THE SIXTH WORD

"It is finished"
(Jn 19:30).

In his gospel, Saint John describes the closing moments of the sad story of Christ's passion and death: "When Jesus had received the wine, he said, 'It is finished.' Then he bowed his head and gave up his spirit" (Jn 19:30).

Thus, before breathing his last, Jesus brought to mind all the sacrifices of the old law (which were indeed figures of his sacrifice on the cross), all the prayers of the patriarchs, all the prophecies about his life and death, all the injuries and insults which had been predicted he would suffer, and seeing that it was all accomplished, said: "It is finished" (Jn 19:30).

In the Letter to the Hebrews, we read: "Let us run with perseverance the race that is set before us, looking to Jesus the pioneer and perfecter of our faith, who for the sake of the joy that was set before him endured the cross, disregarding its shame" (Heb 12:1–2). Thus, we are exhorted to resist temptations with patience until the end, following the example of Jesus who did not leave the cross until he had died on it.

Jesus was determined to complete his sacrifice by dying on the cross in order to convince us that God gives the reward of glory only to those who persevere to the end. "But the one who endures to the end will be saved" (Mt 10:22). For this reason, because of our own weakness, or through the temptations of the devil, when we are tempted to lose patience, or give up in our efforts to please God, let us look to our crucified Savior and remember that we have not yet shed one drop of blood for him.

In the same manner, when we are asked to humble ourselves before others, or control our feelings of resentment towards others, or deny ourselves worldly satisfactions or some other vain curiosity, let us be happy not to deprive our crucified Lord of these kinds of loving gifts. He has not held anything back from us; he has given his life, and all his life's blood. It would be shameful for us to treat him with anything less than total generosity.

In all the trials and tribulations of life, let us follow the example of the saints, especially the martyrs, who accepted and overcame torments and even death. As we read in Romans (8:37): "In all these things we are more than conquerors through him who loved us." Or, to be even more specific, when the devil tempts us, or when we feel spiritually weak, let us trust in the help and merits of Jesus, and say, as we see him dead on the cross: "I can do all things through him who strengthens me" (Phil 4:13).

PRAYER

O my Jesus, you have placed me in this world that I might serve and love you. You have given me so many lights and graces, that I might be faithful to your love. But, unhappy me, how often have I not been willing to lose your grace and turn my back on you. My Jesus, through your own desolate death on the cross, give me strength to be grateful to you during the remainder of my life. From this day on may I drive from my heart any and every affection which is not for you, my Savior and my God.

Mary, my Mother, help me to be faithful to your son who has loved me so much. Amen.

THE SEVENTH WORD

"Father, into your hands I commend my spirit"
(Lk 23:46).

Saint Luke tells us that Jesus cried out these words "with a loud voice." Saint John Chrysostom asserts that Jesus cried out loudly in order to teach us that he died of his own free will, using a strong voice at the very moment he was about to depart this life, to give evidence of his enduring strength.

This, of course, concurs with what Jesus had said earlier, namely, that he would voluntarily sacrifice his life for his sheep, and not die through the malice and ill will of his enemies: "I lay down my life for the sheep…. No one takes it from me, but I lay it down of my own accord" (Jn 10:15, 18).

Saint Athanasius adds that Jesus, by recommending himself to the Father in this way, included in his prayer all the faithful who would obtain salvation through him, because he, as the head, and they, as the members, form one single body. The saint bases this opinion on two statements Jesus made earlier: "Holy Father, protect them in your name that you have given me, so that they may be one, as we are one" and "Father, I desire that those also, whom you have given me, may be with me where I am, to see my glory" (Jn 17:11, 24).

It was this kind of conviction that made Saint Paul affirm his own faith in Jesus: "I know the one in whom I have put my trust" (2 Tim 1:12). Long before Paul, King David had said the same about the future Redeemer: "Into your hands I commit my spirit; you have redeemed me, O LORD, faithful God" (Ps 31:5).

These words of God's servants can and do bring great comfort to the dying at the moment of death, destroying, as they certainly do, the temptations of the devil, as well as any fears which may assail them because of their sins. But let them not wait until they are on their deathbed to recommend themselves to Jesus. Let them do so now, perhaps with the following prayer.

PRAYER

O my Jesus, although I have offended you in the past, do not permit me to turn away from you again in the future. O Lamb of God, sacrificed as a victim of love upon the cross, grant by the merits of your death that I may love you with all my heart and be wholly yours until the end of my days on earth. And when the time comes for me to die, let me die glowing with love for you. Into your hands, O Lord, I commend my spirit.

Mary, my Mother, I trust in your prayers. Pray that I may live and die faithful to your son. To you I say, as did Saint Bonaventure, "In you, O Lady, I have hoped, I shall not be confounded forever." Amen.

Chapter Six

THE DEATH OF JESUS

JESUS DIES AND TRIUMPHS OVER DEATH

S aint John says that Jesus, before breathing his last, bowed his head. He did this as a sign that he, voluntarily and in total humility, accepted death from the hands of his Father. As Saint Paul wrote: "He humbled himself and became obedient to the point of death—even death on a cross" (Phil 2:8).

When Jesus was on the cross, with his hands and feet nailed to this instrument of death, he could not move any part of his body except his head. Saint Athanasius remarks that death did not dare to approach to take life away from the author of life itself; what was needed was his consent, which he gave by bowing his head. Saint Ambrose, commenting on the phrase from Saint Matthew's gospel, "Then Jesus cried again with a loud voice and breathed his last" (or as some versions have it "gave up his spirit") (Mt 27:50), states this proves Jesus was not forced to die, nor did he die because of the violence of his executioners, but because he chose to die to save us from eternal death.

Saint Paul, echoing the words of the prophet Hosea, calls Jesus' death a victory: "Death has been swallowed up in victory. Where, O death, is your victory? Where, O death, is your sting? The sting of death is sin" (1 Cor 15:54–56). Jesus, the Lamb of God, destroyed sin which was the cause of our death. This was Jesus' victory because, by his death, he banished sin and delivered us from eternal death.

The author of the Letter to the Hebrews states: "He [Jesus] likewise shared the same things, so that through death he might destroy the one who the power of death, that is, the devil, and free those who all their lives were held in slavery by the fear of death" (Heb 2:14–15). This was the victory of the cross, on which Jesus, the author of life, died and, by his death, won life for us.

It was for this reason that Saint Francis de Sales wrote: "Let us look upon our divine Savior stretched upon the cross, as upon the altar of his love, and let us cast ourselves in spirit upon the same cross, that we may die with him who has been willing to die for us."

JESUS DEAD UPON THE CROSS

As we contemplate our Redeemer now dead on the cross, let us say to the Eternal Father, in the words of the Psalmist: "O God, look on the face of your anointed" (Ps 84:9).

Yes, eternal Father, look upon your only-begotten Son who, in order to satisfy your will that those who were lost should be saved, came down upon earth, took on our human nature as well as all of our afflictions except sin. In short, after making himself one of us, he lived among us as the poorest, the most despised, the most tormented of all. At the end of his life, he was condemned to death, and during his trials, his flesh was torn by scourging, his head was crowned with thorns, his hands and feet were pierced with nails, fastening him to a cross.

Thus, for the three hours he hung upon this tree of utter anguish, he was despised and derided as a false prophet, blasphemed as a sacrilegious impostor for claiming he was your Son, until he finally died a terrible and desolate death.

Tell us, Eternal Father, what fault did your Son commit to deserve so horrible a punishment? You know his innocence, his holiness; why did you treat him so? Ah, I hear your reply, already spoken by the prophet Isaiah: "He was...stricken for the transgression of my people" (Isa 53:8). I reply, he did not, could not, deserve to be punished, for he was innocence and holiness itself. You continue, the punishment was due to you for your sins. But in order that I might not see you lost eternally, my beloved creature, I gave my divine Son such a miserable life and desolate death. Think, my child, of the excessive love I have for you! Remember the words of the gospel: "For God so loved the world that he gave his only Son, so that everyone who believes in him may not perish but may have eternal life" (Jn 3:16). Or, as Saint Paul asserted: "Live in love, as Christ loved us and gave himself up for us, a fragrant offering and sacrifice to God" (Eph 5:2).

What the Death of Jesus Accomplished for Us

Through the sacrifice of the cross, Jesus, acting as both priest and victim, redeemed us. He made it possible for us to get to heaven after we die.

In fact, he stripped death of all its terrors. Before his own death on the cross, death was considered to be little more than a punishment for rebels. But, by the merits of Jesus, death became a sacrifice so precious that, when we unite our death to that of Jesus, it makes us worthy to enjoy the same glory that God enjoys. It gives us hope that, some day, we will hear him say: "Enter into the joy of your master" (Mt 25:21).

Thus death, heretofore an object of pain and dread, now, through the death of Jesus, is changed. What had been feared as a blind passing into a state of unknown dangers now becomes a sweet passage into security and eternal bliss, the boundless delights of paradise.

It was for this reason that the saints no longer regarded death with fear, but with joy and desire. Saint Augustine says that those who love Jesus crucified, live with patience and die with joy. And we note that, as a general rule, those who in life have been the most troubled by persecutions, temptations, and other painful experiences, are the ones who are most comfortable and peaceful at the hour of death.

Sometimes good people are fearful at the time of their death, but this happens because the Lord wishes to increase their merits. The more painful death is to them, the greater the sacrifice and the more acceptable it becomes to God, and accordingly, the more profitable for them in eternity.

For the holy people of the Old Testament, before the sacrifice of Jesus on the cross, death was a difficult experience. Jesus had not yet come, yet these good persons sighed for his coming. They waited for his promises, not knowing, however, when they would be fulfilled. At the same time, the devil had great power on earth, and heaven remained closed.

But, as we have seen, through the death of our Redeemer,

hell was conquered, grace abounded, God the Father was reconciled with his children, and paradise was opened and remains open to all who die in God's grace. And if some of these people do not immediately enter into heaven, it is only due to certain faults of which they are not yet cleansed.

Let us then, dear readers, while we are still in exile, not look upon death as a misfortune, but as the end of our pilgrimage, a pilgrimage that still remains so full of dangers and difficulties. Let us see death as the beginning of our eternal happiness which we hope to achieve through the merits of Jesus. And while we continue to think about heaven, let us detach ourselves, as much as possible, from earthly things which may cause us to lose heaven and, instead, be punished in hell.

Let us offer ourselves to God, declaring that we wish to die when God wishes it, as God wishes it, and because God wishes it, praying always that we will depart from this life in God's grace.

PRAYER

O my Jesus, my Savior, I place myself in the arms of your mercy. I have deserved to be in hell for my many sins, but you, instead of punishing me for these offenses, have called me to repentance. I hope that by now you have pardoned me, but if you have not, I ask for pardon now in deepest sorrow. Pardon me, my Jesus, and give me the grace to love you with all my strength until death. And when I reach the end of my life here on earth, make me die burning with love for you, so that I may go on to love you forever. I unite my death to your holy death, by which I hope to be saved, and I say to you in the words of the Psalmist: "In you, O LORD, I seek refuge; do not let me ever be put to shame; in your righteousness deliver me" (Ps 31:1).

And you, Mary, great Mother of God, next to Jesus you are my hope; let me not be confounded forever. Amen.

Chapter Seven

God's Love for Us As Shown in Jesus' Passion and Death

God So Loved Us That He Gave His Own Son to Redeem Us

Saint Francis de Sales called Calvary the "mount of lovers," and claimed that the story of Christ's passion and death is the most powerful incentive for loving him. In order to understand at least partially (we will never be able to understand it fully) the love which God showed toward us in the passion and death of Jesus, we need to look into the Scriptures.

When speaking about holy love, Jesus said: "For God so loved the world that he gave his only Son" (Jn 3:16). The word "so" is important. It indicates that, by giving his Son, God showed us a love which we can never fully comprehend. Because of sin, we were all dead, having lost the life of grace. But the Eternal Father, to make his goodness known, and to show how much he loved us, chose to send his Son to our earth so that by his death, he might restore the life which we had lost. As Saint John wrote:

"God's love was revealed among us in this way: God sent his only Son into the world so that we might live through him" (1 Jn 4:9).

In order to pardon us, God refused pardon to his own Son, desiring that he should be the one who would satisfy divine justice for all our sins. As Saint Paul wrote: "He who did not withhold his own Son, but gave him up for all of us, will he not with him also give us everything else?" (Rom 8:32). The Father "gave him up" into the hands of the executioners that they might load him with insults and torments until he died in agony on the cross. "He did not withhold his own Son."

It was as Isaiah had prophesied: "He was wounded for our transgressions, crushed for our iniquities; upon him was the punishment that made us whole, and by his bruises we are healed" (Isa 53:5). This overwhelming love God has for us was confirmed by Saint Paul who wrote: "But God, who is rich in mercy, out of the great love with which he loved us even when we were dead through our trespasses, made us alive together with Christ...and raised us up with him" (Eph 2:4–6).

Yes, says the Apostle, God has done so much for us that if we were not assured of it by faith, no one could ever imagine it possible. As the Church in the Easter Vigil liturgy proclaims: "Father, how wonderful your care for us! How boundless your merciful love! To ransom a slave you gave away your Son."

God, who is love, loves all his creatures: "For you love all things that exist, and detest none of the things that you have made" (Wis 11:24). But the love that God bears to us seems to be his best and dearest love. In fact, God seems to have preferred us even to the angels, since he was willing to die for us, but not for the fallen angels.

THE SON OF GOD OFFERED HIMSELF OUT OF LOVE FOR US

Therefore, when we speak of the love Jesus has for us, we must keep in mind that, on the one hand, he saw that we were lost through sin, and, on the other, divine justice required perfect satisfaction for our offenses. He alone could make adequate reparation, so he voluntarily offered to do so. As Scripture says: "He bore the sin of many, and made intercession for the transgressors" (Isa 53:12).

Thus, Isaiah's prophecy is fulfilled when he says: "He was oppressed, and he was afflicted, yet he did not open his mouth; like a lamb that is led to the slaughter, and like a sheep that before its shearers is silent, so he did not open his mouth" (Isa 53:7). Saint Paul paints the picture of a submissive Christ: "He humbled himself and became obedient to the point of death— even death on a cross" (Phil 2:8). But let us not conclude that Jesus died only to obey his Father; he chose to die because he loved us, as he himself had declared: "I am the good shepherd... I lay down my life for the sheep.... No one takes it from me, but I lay it down of my own accord" (Jn 10:14, 15, 18). As Saint Paul testifies: "Christ loved us and gave himself up for us, a fragrant offering and sacrifice to God" (Eph 5:2).

Jesus spoke about the kind of death he would suffer: "And I, when I am lifted up from the earth, will draw all people to myself" (Jn 12:32). Saint John Chrysostom says that Jesus draws these "people" away from the hands of a tyrant, namely the devil, who keeps sinners enslaved and in chains, only to torment them later, forever in hell.

Think of how miserable our destiny would have been had

Jesus not died for us! We all would have been sent to hell for all eternity, but Jesus saved us by shedding his blood for us on the cross. He did not redeem us with gold or any other earthly treasure; to the contrary, he saved us by dying for us. The kings and other rulers of this world send their subjects to die in wars to preserve their own security; Jesus, for his part, chose to die in order to save us, his creatures.

JESUS DIED FOR EACH OF US

Saint Augustine, contemplating Jesus crucified, comments: "O, what an unbelievable thing! To see the Judge judged, to see justice condemned, to see life dying!" These extraordinary things happened solely because of the love Jesus had for us. As we read in the Scriptures: he "loves us and freed us from our sins by his blood" (Rev 1:5).

"O power of love!" cries Saint Bernard. "The God of all is made lowest of all! What accomplished this? Love, forgetful of its own dignity, love triumphant over divinity. God who can be conquered by no one causes himself to be conquered by the love he bears for us."

But this love is not just for people in general. We must remember that whatever Jesus suffered in his passion and death, he suffered for each of us individually. This is what Saint Paul taught when he wrote: "And the life I now live in the flesh I live by faith in the Son of God, who loved me and gave himself for me" (Gal 2:20). Saint Augustine says to God: "You have loved me…more than yourself, since in order to deliver me from death, you have been willing to die for me." He goes on to state that the sufferings of Jesus proved that "his mercy exceeded our sins."

Truly, Jesus could have saved us by shedding just one single drop of his blood, so why did he pour it all out in such a painful death? Saint Bernard says it was because of love: "What a drop might have done he chose to do with a stream, in order to show us the excessive love he bore us."

PRAYER

O Eternal God, I have dishonored you by my sins, but Jesus, through his death, has more than abundantly restored the honor due to you. For the love of Jesus, then, have mercy on me. And you Jesus, my Redeemer, grant that from now on I may love you in gratitude for your love for me. I have deserved to be condemned to hell, and to be unable to love you any more. But, O my Jesus, give me any punishment but this. Cause me to love you, and then chastise me as you will. Deprive me of everything, except yourself.

O holy Virgin Mary, help me with your prayers. Mother of mercy, obtain for me that I may never cease to love Jesus, your son and my Savior. Amen.

Chapter Eight

WE PLACE ALL OUR HOPES IN THE MERITS OF JESUS

JESUS CHRIST CRUCIFIED: OUR HOPE IN ALL OUR NEEDS

Saint Peter, preaching about Jesus on the first Pentecost, told the people gathered in Jerusalem: "There is salvation in no one else" (Acts 4:12). He was demonstrating that Jesus, by his death on the cross and resurrection from that death, gives us hope for any and every blessing from God, as long as we are faithful to his commands.

Saint John Chrysostom wrote about the cross of Jesus in these words: "The cross is the hope of Christians, the staff for those who are crippled, the comfort of the poor, the defeat of the proud, the victory over the demons, the guide for youth, the refuge for those who are in danger, the teacher of the just, rest for the afflicted, a physician for the sick, and the glory of the martyrs."

Let us enlarge upon this quote by saying that the cross, or more properly Jesus crucified, truly is

- The *hope* of all Christians, for if we did not have Jesus we could not expect salvation.
- The *staff* for those who are disabled, because in our present state, we are all disabled. We would not be able to walk the way of salvation without the help of the graces won by Jesus.
- The *comfort* of the poor. On our own we are poor, and whatever we have comes from Jesus.
- The *defeat* of the proud, for true followers of Jesus cannot be proud after seeing him condemned to die on the cross as a villain and an evildoer.
- The *victory* over the demons, for the very sign of the cross is enough to drive them from us.
- The *guide* for youth, because those who are beginning to walk in the ways of God learn much from the cross.
- The *refuge* for those in danger and for those in danger of perishing because of strong temptations; they find strength through the cross.
- The *teacher* of the just, for how many saints have learned wisdom from the cross, and from bearing the troubles of this life.
- The *rest* for the afflicted, for where can they find greater relief than from contemplating the cross on which a God suffers out of love for them?
- The *physician* for the sick, for when these embrace the cross, the wounds of their soul are healed.
- The *glory* of the martyrs, for to die like Jesus, the King of Martyrs, is the greatest glory they can ever possess.

Saint Bernard says that God makes those who hope in Jesus all-powerful, and adds that, as long as they do not trust solely in their own strength, they will be able to conquer all evil. No force, no fiction, can overcome or deceive them.

Saint Paul wrote these words about the cross: "For the message about the cross is foolishness to those who are perishing, but to us who are being saved it is the power of God" (1 Cor 1:18). Thus, the Apostle warns us not to follow those who put their trust in riches, or relatives, or worldly friends, or those who consider the saints fools for not seeking these earthly goods. Rather, he says we ought to place all our hopes in the love of the cross, in Jesus crucified, since he gives every blessing possible to those who trust in him.

The power and strength of the world is different from that of God. For worldly people, power and strength consist of riches and honors; but in the eyes of God, power and strength come from humility and endurance. This is why Saint Augustine says that our strength comes from knowing that we are weak, and humbly admitting it. He echoes Saint Jerome who said that our perfection in this life consists of knowing that we are imperfect, for then we will distrust our own strength and instead abandon ourselves to God who protects and saves those who hope in him. As David wrote: "He is a shield for all who take refuge in him" (Ps 18:30).

When Jesus took the weakness of human nature upon himself, he merited for us the strength to overcome our weakness. As the writer of the Letter to the Hebrews points out: "Because he himself was tested by what he suffered, he is able to help those who are being tested" (Heb 2:18).

This means that Jesus, having been afflicted by temptations, is more ready to empathize with us and help us when we are tempted. As we read in that same letter: "For we do not have a high priest who is unable to sympathize with our weaknesses, but we have one who in every respect has been tested as we are, yet without sin. Let us therefore approach the throne of grace with boldness, so that we may receive mercy and find grace to help in time of need" (Heb 4:15–16).

These words, in addition to what the evangelists tell us in the gospels, bear witness to the fact that Jesus can and will help us in the circumstances and trials of our own life. In the garden of Gethsemane, Jesus endured fears, weaknesses, and sorrows, and merited for us the courage to resist the threats of those who would do us harm. From him, we also receive the strength to overcome the weariness we experience in praying, or practicing mortifications, or performing other devout exercises. He also won for us the power to endure with peace of mind the natural disappointment we feel when things go wrong.

We should also recall that in Gethsemane Jesus foresaw the sufferings and painful death he was about to endure, yet he nevertheless chose to suffer this human weakness. "The spirit indeed is willing, but the flesh is weak" (Mt 26:41). In truth, he prayed that the cup of suffering might pass from him, but quickly added: "Yet not what I want but what you want" (Mt 26:39). The Scriptures tell us that he repeatedly prayed to the Father: "Your will be done…your will be done."

These loving words from Jesus won for all Christians the grace to be resigned to God's holy will in times of adversity. They also gave to the holy martyrs and confessors the strength to resist the persecutions and torments of tyrants. This is what Saint Leo taught in his book about the sufferings and death of

Jesus. He says that Jesus came to earth to take our infirmities and weaknesses upon himself and to give us in return his own strength and constancy.

This had particularly been true in the early years of the Church when the martyrs accepted, with patience and even joy, the most cruel torments. Saint Ignatius the martyr, for example, who was condemned to be thrown to the wild animals to be killed by them, wrote this in a letter to the Roman authorities: "Suffer me, my children, to be ground down by the teeth of wild beasts, that I may become wheat for my Redeemer. I seek only him who died for me. He who is the only object of my love was crucified for me, and the love I bear to him makes me desire to be crucified for him." And of Saint Lawrence the martyr it is said that while he was being burned to death, the flames which attacked his body from without, were less hot than the flames of love which burned within his heart. Such was the patience and fortitude which many other martyrs later gained from the passion and death of Jesus.

The courage to be received from the Crucified Jesus was not lost on Saint Paul, as this celebrated passage from his Letter to the Romans affirms: "Who will separate us from the love of Christ? Will hardship, or distress, or persecution, or famine, or nakedness, or peril, or sword? ...No, in all these things we are more than conquerors through him who loved us" (Rom 8:35, 37).

The first object of our hope is eternal blessedness, the "fruition of God," as Saint Thomas calls it, which means our perfect enjoyment of God in heaven. We can and must hope that all the means necessary for acquiring this gift, such as the pardon of our sins, final perseverance, and a good death, will come to us, not from our own strength or merits, or even our good resolutions, but solely from the merits of Jesus our Savior. If we look only to Jesus for these graces, we can be confident of getting to heaven.

OUR HOPE THAT THE SACRIFICE OF JESUS WILL TAKE AWAY OUR SINS

John the Baptist, announcing the arrival of Jesus to his own followers, used these words: "Here is the Lamb of God who takes away the sin of the world!" (Jn 1:29). Both Isaiah and Jeremiah had used that same word, "lamb," to refer to Jesus, the former saying that he was "like a lamb that is led to the slaughter" (Isa 53:7), and the latter, declaring: "[he] was like a gentle lamb led to the slaughter" (Jer 11:19).

In the Jewish religious tradition, lambs were sacrificed often, sometimes daily, and the paschal lamb was a particularly important symbol. But all these sacrificed lambs could not take away a single sin; they served only to represent the sacrifice of the divine Lamb, Jesus, who with his own blood would wash away our sins and the punishment due for them.

Isaiah wrote: "The LORD has laid on him the iniquity of us all" (Isa 53:6). Saint Peter describes how this happened: "He himself bore our sins in his body on the cross, so that, free from sins, we might live for righteousness; by his wounds you have been healed" (1 Pet 2:24). Saint Bonaventure reflected on this and exclaimed: "What can be more wonderful than that wounds should heal, and death give life?"

Saint Paul describes the special blessings we receive from Jesus in these words: "In him [Jesus] we have redemption through his blood, the forgiveness of our trespasses, according to the riches of his grace that he lavished on us" (Eph 1:7–8). In the Letter to the Hebrews, we read how this "redemption" took place: "When Christ came as a high priest…he entered once for all into the Holy Place, not with the blood of goats and calves, but with his own blood, thus obtaining eternal redemption. For if the blood of goats and bulls…sanctifies those who have been defiled so that their flesh is purified, how much more will the blood of Christ who…offered himself without blemish to God, purify our conscience from dead works to worship the living God! For this reason he is the mediator of a new covenant" (Heb 9:11–15).

Because of the sin of Adam, the whole human race entered into a fallen state, and passed into disfavor with God. Divine justice, now offended by sin, needed to be satisfied, but this could be done only through a divine person acting in our stead. Jesus, as mediator between God and us, offered to pay, with his blood and through his death, the debt owed to God, in order to reconcile us with the Father. This reconciliation was very often prefigured in the Old Testament by the sacrifices of animals, and by many other related symbolic actions and objects. For example, the altars, the tabernacle in the temple, and the ark of the Covenant contain the showbreads and the tablets of the law. All these things, and many other similar objects, were signs and figures of the promised redemption which would finally and fully be accomplished by the sacred blood of Jesus being poured forth on the altar of the cross. This was how Jesus established the eternal covenant between the Father and us, his children, and won our pardon and salvation.

This is what Jesus alluded to and confirmed, on the very night before he died, when he instituted the holy Eucharist. As Saint Matthew records it: "He [Jesus] took a cup, and after giving thanks he gave it to them [the apostles], saying, 'Drink from it, all of you; for this is my blood of the covenant, which is poured out for many for the forgiveness of sins'" (Mt 26:27–28). He used the term "poured out" because he was about to shed not just a part of his blood, but all of it, in satisfaction for our sins and to obtain our pardon.

Jesus' great sacrifice on the cross, which is presented anew in each holy Mass, has the power to forever save those who approach the Father in faith and good works. For, as both Saint Ambrose and Saint Augustine attest, it is this same sacrifice that Jesus continues to offer to the Father for our lasting benefit. Through it, Jesus also continues to be our advocate, mediator, and priest, making intercession for us, as we read in the Letter to the Hebrews: "He is able for all time to save those who approach God through him, since he always lives to make intercession for them" (Heb 7:25).

OUR HOPE FOR FINAL PERSEVERANCE THROUGH THE SACRIFICE OF JESUS

In order to persevere in goodness until our death, we cannot trust solely in our resolutions or our promises to God; for if we rely on our strength, we are lost. Our hope for perseverance must be placed in Jesus, who will help us overcome all attacks from our enemies, in this world and the next.

Sometimes, God allows even his saints either to feel downhearted, or to become fearful and afraid. The great Saint Paul tells us that this happened to him at one stage of his life: "We do

not want you to be unaware, brothers and sisters, of the afflic-
tion we experienced in Asia; for we were so utterly, unbearably
crushed that we despaired of life itself" (2 Cor 1:8). In the next
verse, however, he explains why this happened: "Indeed, we felt
that we had received the sentence of death so that we would rely
not on ourselves but on God who raises the dead" (2 Cor 1:9).

Later, in the same letter, he expands about why he trusted
wholly in God: "We are afflicted in every way, but not crushed;
perplexed, but not driven to despair; persecuted, but not forsaken; struck down, but not destroyed; always carrying in the
body the death of Jesus, so that the life of Jesus may also be
made visible in our bodies" (2 Cor 4:8–10). The lesson is very
clear: even though we are weak and prone to lose the treasure of
God's grace, our ability to hold onto this grace comes from God.
"We have this treasure in clay jars [earthen vessels], so that it
may be made clear that this extraordinary power belongs to God
and does not come from us" (2 Cor 4:7).

Even though all our strength to live without sin and do good
works truly comes from God, we must still be on guard not to
make ourselves weaker than we are naturally. Our spiritual frailty
will be evident if, or when, we pay little or no attention to small
faults: for example, faults such as taking pride in superior learn-
ing, or our higher station in life; or seeking superfluous pleasures, wishing to please everyone, or becoming resentful when
others pay little attention to us. Or again not always telling the
truth, murmuring under our breath against other people, showing aversion towards others, or even attacking them about small
things. And, of course, gossiping about them.

We must remember that every attachment to earthly things,
every act of inordinate self-love, serves to drag us down to the

point that we eventually will be deprived of the divine help needed to avoid serious sin. This can, of course, become a very dangerous situation. But if we pray, pray hard and pray always, we shall obtain the graces we need, and persevere until the end.

There can be no doubt that God promises us eternal salvation and everlasting happiness through the merits of Jesus sacrificed on the cross, and risen from the dead. Saint Paul wrote: "For you did not receive a spirit of slavery to fall back into fear, but you have received a spirit of adoption. When we cry 'Abba! Father!' it is that very Spirit bearing witness with our spirit that we are children of God, and if children, then heirs, heirs of God and joint heirs with Christ—if, in fact, we suffer with him so that we may also be glorified with him" (Rom 8:15–17).

Jesus is our captain; he goes before us with his standard, which is the cross. We must follow him, each of us bearing our own cross, just as Jesus proclaimed: "If any want to become my followers, let them deny themselves and take up their cross and follow me" (Mt 16:24).

In this respect, Saint Paul also exhorts us to suffer with courage, strengthened by the hope of paradise: "I consider that the sufferings of this present time are not worth comparing with the glory about to be revealed to us" (Rom 8:18). We do not, as yet, enjoy the glory, because we are not yet saved. We have not yet finished our life in the grace of God. But Saint Paul also tells us that hope in the merits of Jesus will save us: "In hope we [are] saved" (Rom 8:24). Jesus will not fail to give us every help for our salvation if we are faithful to him and pray.

If perhaps we fear that we might not know how to pray, Saint Paul again tells us not to worry: "The Spirit helps us in our weakness; for we do not know how to pray as we ought, but that very Spirit intercedes with sighs too deep for words…. We know that all things work together for good for those who love God" (Rom 8:26, 28).

And if we still might be inclined to fear or despair because of our sins, we have one more assurance to give us confidence. It again comes from Saint Paul: "If God is for us, who is against us? He who did not withhold his own Son, but gave him up for all of us, will he not with him also give us everything else? Who will bring any charge against God's elect? It is God who justifies. Who is to condemn? It is Christ Jesus, who died, yes, who was raised, who is at the right hand of God, who indeed intercedes for us" (Rom 8:31–34).

PRAYER

O my Jesus, if I look at my sins, I am ashamed to be asking for paradise, for I have sinned so much. But when I look at you upon the cross, I cannot cease to hope for heaven, knowing that you were willing to die on the cross to atone for my sins, and to win heaven for me. O my sweet Redeemer, I hope through the merits of your death and resurrection, that you have already pardoned me. I repent of all my sins, and I ask for the grace never to sin again.

O Mary, hope of sinners, help me with my prayers. Pray for me, now and always, and especially at the hour of my death. Amen.

Chapter Nine

THE RESURRECTION OF JESUS

We cannot end this book leaving Jesus hanging dead on the cross, where he suffered and died for our sins on the first Good Friday. The redemption story does not, cannot, end on Calvary. No, it too must be taken down from the cross as Jesus was, and placed, for a while, in the darkness of the tomb. But the story, again like Jesus, cannot remain buried. For Jesus, the tomb was only a temporary venue. He remained there only until that first Easter Sunday morning when, like a bursting sun, he rose from it to a new and glorious life. It is for this reason the Redemption story must have its climax in the fact that Jesus was restored to life and now continues to live for all eternity.

Not so long ago, theologians used to study the Redemption story without mentioning the Resurrection at all. The fact of Easter was indeed cited for its value as a part of apologetics; but few, if any, theologians considered it to be an integral part of the inexhaustible mystery of salvation. It was as though only the Incarnation mattered; we are saved because God became man and lived among us, and then died on the cross for our sins.

The Resurrection, when reference was made to it, was not cited as a part of our salvation as much as it was used to show the personal triumph of Jesus over his enemies. They had made him suffer an excruciating death, but by his resurrection, he overcame it, and as one Easter hymn put it, "now he lives, no more to die. Alleluia!"

We do not know exactly why and how this happened, but we do know that from the 1900s onward, theologians have been hard at work showing how Jesus' resurrection is an integral part of God's plan for our salvation. One of these theologians is Father Francis Xavier Durrwell, a European Redemptorist, whose classic treatise on the Resurrection showed that this mystery represents not only Jesus' triumph over death and sin, but it also is a pledge of salvation for Christian believers. The Resurrection, says Father Durrwell, proves that the vital center of our life is not the cross of suffering and defeat, but the victory symbolized by the open tomb.[1]

Why and how is this true? For one answer to this question, we need to go to Saint Paul, who expressed it clearly and forcefully when writing to his converts. This is particularly seen in the following three statements:

If Christ has not been raised, your faith is futile and you are still in your sins (1 Cor 15:17).

And [Christ] died for all…and was raised for them (2 Cor 5:15).

Jesus our Lord…who was handed over to death for our trespasses and was raised for our justification (Rom 4:24, 25).

This truth, underlined in these statements, may have possibly prompted some pastors to add a fifteenth station to the Way of the Cross in their churches: Jesus Rises from the Dead. This is a significant indication that the event of the Resurrection is part of the mystery of Redemption, not an epilogue to it. It was this truth that Pope John Paul II was quick to emphasize in his Jubilee 2000 visit to the Holy Land when he quietly corrected a speaker who referred to the *fourteen* stations of the *Via Crucis*. "There are fifteen," said the Holy Father in a low voice.

Of course, the Church has, from the beginning of its existence, believed that Jesus arose from the dead. This is a primary and basic belief, the cornerstone of the Christian faith. As the new *Catechism of the Catholic Church* states: "The Resurrection of Jesus is the crowning truth of our faith in Christ, a faith believed and lived as the central truth by the first Christian community; handed on as fundamental by Tradition; established by the documents of the New Testament; and preached as an essential part of the Paschal mystery along with the cross" (CCC 638).

The saga of the Resurrection is found in all of the gospels, and is repeatedly referred to in the Acts of the Apostles. The story of Christ being raised from the dead was the basis of Peter's preaching to the people in Jerusalem on Pentecost. He referred to the Resurrection in clear terms when speaking about the crucified Jesus who was "freed from death," "this Jesus [whom] God raised up, and of that all of us are witnesses" (Acts 2:32).

The apostles, as well other followers of Jesus, had indeed witnessed the miracle of the Resurrection. The person whom they had seen dead on the cross now walked again among them, very much alive and perfectly real. The one who had been buried in a tomb is now asking for food, sharing with them the fresh fish which they had just caught from the lake. It was this same Jesus who suddenly appeared to them in the upper room, even though the doors were locked, to show them, particularly to the doubting Thomas, the wounds on his hands and side, even asking that these wounds be subjected to the touch of those who might still be in doubt.

This miraculous drama continued for some forty days, until the Ascension. During this entire time, Jesus was as real as a man of flesh and blood, although his body manifested supernatural gifts not belonging to this earth. During this time, however, his attitude and teachings followed closely, and in some instances word for word, what he had previously taught them, particularly when he spoke of the primacy of love. He urged his disciples to "go and teach all nations," and renewed his promise to be with them always: "Remember, I am with you always, to the end of the age" (Mt 28:20).

It is ultimately the Scriptures that help us understand the intimate and necessary relationship between the life, death, *and* resurrection of Jesus as well as our own eternal destiny. In dealing with the earlier periods of Jesus' life, the synoptic gospels (Matthew, Mark, and Luke), do not emphasize the resurrection of Jesus as much as his role as the herald of the kingdom and leader of the people. In the earlier part of the story, he is portrayed more as the prophet, and in order to become his follower, all someone had to do was repent, convert, believe, and live a life in conformity to the Sermon on the Mount.

However, as the gospel narratives unfold, a new element enters as an integral part of his mission. Jesus begins to talk to his disciples about the necessity of his upcoming death. It becomes clearer that his death is part of the messianic scheme. He told them in clear terms: "the Son of Man came...to give his life a ransom for many" (Mk 10:45).

As a result, a second theme appears. The disciples must unite themselves to him and his destiny, so that, having lost their lives for his sake, they might find them again when he returned in the glory of the kingdom (see Mt 16:24–28).

Finally, a third theme appears. It serves as a link between the first two and involves the Resurrection, closely connected to the twofold mission of Jesus, which is to announce the kingdom and die for many. It must be noted that in the three solemn predictions of the passion which the Synoptics give us, the Resurrection comes as the crowning point in Christ's life. Jesus demonstrates a threefold rhythm for his destiny: the Son of Man is rejected by his people and handed over to the Gentiles; he is tortured, humbled, and killed; and he rises on the third day.

Thus, Jesus' resurrection is not only meant to be the last act in the story of his passion and death and to brighten the picture by a gleam of light. In Jesus' eyes, his resurrection was as much a part of his mission as was his death. It was a part of his messianic destiny: the Son of Man must die and then rise again. "Thus it is written, that the Messiah is to suffer and to rise from the dead on the third day" (Lk 24:46).

In fact, this is the truth which Jesus explained to the two disciples who met him on the way to Emmaus, at eventide on the very day of his resurrection. They were saddened by all that had happened to Jesus, in whom they had put so much trust. Now he was dead, the victim of a crucifixion, and their hopes had died with him. But it was Jesus who grouped his death, glory, and resurrection together. As he said to them: "Was it not necessary that the Messiah should suffer these things and then enter into his glory?" (Lk 24:26).

The fourth evangelist, John, takes a slightly different path but arrives at the same place as the other three. In his gospel, John's original emphasis is on the divinity of Jesus, as can be seen from the opening words: "In the beginning was the Word, and the Word was with God, and the Word was God" (Jn 1:1).

Early in his gospel, John portrays Jesus as the one who brings both life and light: "Whoever believes in the Son has eternal life" (Jn 3:36). Redemption is seen as already being completed by the Incarnation and faith. But as we continue our study of his gospel, we see that to some degree, John strays from the "life and light" elements of Jesus, and more into his corporeality, Jesus' "bodiliness." John is both the most heavenly and the most earthly of the evangelists. He shows how sublime the sources of our salvation are: first, the very bosom of the Father from whence came the Word, and then, secondly, the manner in which the life of this Word was sacrificed for us, through the destruction of Jesus' body in his bloody death on the cross. Thus, he links the whole process to the paschal mystery, and Jesus is the paschal lamb by whose blood we are both marked and saved.

For Saint Paul however the case was clear. More than anyone else, Saint Paul is the apostle of the risen Lord. He is the primary "witness to the Resurrection." He has seen and heard the Lord Jesus in his heavenly glory, and only in that way. The Jesus whom he met transcended the limitations of history. The Jesus he knew was already glorified; in fact, that is how Paul first met him, on the road to Damascus.

It is for this reason that Paul preached not as much about Jesus' words and deeds, which had been handed down by tradition, but rather about his own realization of the resurrected Lord, the source of our redemption. Jesus' resurrection from the dead was the primary truth that mattered to Paul. He sees Jesus as the source of life, but it is the risen Jesus that he sees.

That is the reason, at the beginning of this chapter, we listed three important quotations from Saint Paul. If we read them over, again and again, and try to discover their deepest meanings, we will surely come to an even greater appreciation of the mystery of Jesus' resurrection, and how it affects our life and eternal salvation. Those who wish to delve even further into this matter are invited to read Father Durrwell's classic book which is cited at the end of this chapter. This will certainly lead them into the long neglected but vital lessons of the resurrection of the Lord Jesus.

1. Father Francis Xavier Durrwell's book, *The Resurrection: A Biblical Study*, was translated by Rosemary Sheed and published by Sheed & Ward in 1960.

Meditations on the
Passion of Jesus

SUNDAY

❦

The Love of Jesus in Suffering for Us

Ever since the coming of Jesus on earth, we no longer live in a time of fear, but in a time of love. This is because God has seen fit to die for us. "Live in love, as Christ loved us and gave himself up for us" (Eph 5:2).

Before the Word was made flesh, we might have wondered if God really loved us with a tender kind of love. But after seeing Jesus suffer a bloody and ignominious death on the cross for us, we can have no doubts about God's love. How can we ever comprehend the excess of love with which God the Son paid for our sins! Yet, it is true that he did love us with infinite love. The Scriptures affirm it: "Surely he has borne our infirmities and carried our diseases; ...he was wounded for our transgressions, crushed for our iniquities; upon him was the punishment that made us whole, and by his bruises we are healed" (Isa 53:4–5).

In the Book of Revelation, we read of Jesus as one "who loves us and freed us from our sins by his blood" (Rev 1:5). He was willing to shed all his blood to make it, as it were, our bath of salvation. O infinite mercy! O infinite love of a God which truly obliges us to love in return!

But it is important to remember that what should most inflame our hearts is not so much the actual death of Jesus, nor the pains and ignominies he suffered for us, but the motive behind his passion and death. He did it all out of love; he suffered and died to win our hearts. As Saint John wrote: "We know love by this, that he laid down his life for us" (1 Jn 3:16).

It was not at all necessary for Jesus to suffer so much and die in order to save us. He could have saved us by shedding only one drop of blood, or even a single tear. Either one of these acts could save a thousand worlds. But he willed to pour out all his blood, he willed to lose his life in a sea of sorrows and contempt to make us understand his great love, and oblige us to love him in return. Saint Paul writes: "the love of Christ urges us on" (2 Cor 5:14). It is not just Jesus' sufferings, nor his death, but his love which calls and compels us to love him.

In the same passage, Saint Paul writes: "He died for all, so that those who live might live no longer for themselves, but for him who died and was raised for them" (2 Cor 5:15). Jesus, indeed, is full of love for us, but are we full of love for him? We say we want to express our ability to love, but where, and on whom do we most our bestow love? For some of us, it is on riches, others on honors or pleasures, others on relatives and friends, and some others even bestow their choicest love on animals! How few are those who show that they truly wish to only love God above every other good.

How can we best enkindle the fire of true love for God in our hearts? Saint Bonaventure answers: through the wounds of Jesus, which are like darts to pierce stony hearts, or like flames to set the coldest of souls on fire. For a person who believes in, and meditates on, the passion of Jesus, it is impossible to offend God, or not love him almost to the extent of madness, especially when they see that God is crazy in love with us. "We have seen," Saint Lawrence Justinian said, "wisdom infatuated by too much love."

Saint Paul tells of the reaction of his audiences when he preached about Jesus crucified. "We proclaim Christ crucified, a stumbling block to Jews and foolishness to Gentiles" (1 Cor 1:23). The Gentiles could not understand this divine lunacy. How could an all-powerful and all-happy God, they asked, be willing to die for his creatures? And we, who have received the gift of faith, must also ask: how is it possible for us not to deeply love this God who has loved us so much? As the old adage tells it: love must be repaid with love.

PRAYER

O my Jesus, by your cross, by your wounds, by your death, you bind me to love you with all my heart. Help me to love you and to please you by my life here on earth so that I may live with you forever in heaven.

Mary, my hope, pray to Jesus for me. Amen.

MONDAY

THE AGONY OF JESUS IN THE GARDEN

As the hour for his death approached, Jesus went into the garden of Gethsemane. There, he began to prepare for the cruel sufferings and horrible death that awaited him. The gospel writer tells us what happened: He "began to be distressed and agitated" (Mk 14:33).

Without a doubt, what Jesus felt at this time was a fear of death and a feeling of deepest sorrow, as he foresaw the scourging, thorns, nails, and the cross. He also saw the desolate death which he would endure, abandoned on the cross, lacking all comfort, both human and divine. Terrified by the visions of these sufferings, Jesus asked his Eternal Father to be freed of them: "My Father, if it is possible, let this cup pass from me" (Mt 26:39).

What is happening? Is this not the same Jesus who had been so ready and willing to die for us? Had he not, earlier in his life, proclaimed: "I have a baptism with which to be baptized, and what stress I am under until it is completed!" How, then, can he fear these pains and this death?

He was, without a doubt, willing to die for us. But throughout his dreadful agony in the garden, he showed himself fearful and grieved so that we might not suppose that, since he was divine, his death would be without pain. No, he wanted us to understand that, not only was he willing to die for us, but also that his death would be so horrible that it would frighten him intensely, even before it happened.

As he entered Gethsemane, Jesus told his disciples: "I am deeply grieved, even to death" (Mt 26:38). He could have delivered himself, saved himself, from the impending tragedy, for after all, he was still God. But no, he knew that sufferings awaited him; it was not so much these sufferings that caused him grief, for they were the price he was willing to pay to save us. What caused such grief in Jesus' heart was knowing that, even after his passion and death, sins would still be committed throughout the world.

This was the vision that confronted him and made him sad: "deeply grieved, even to death," so much so that "his sweat became like great drops of blood falling down on the ground" (Lk 22:44). Jesus saw all the sins which human beings were going to commit even after his death, all the hatred, impurities, thefts, sacrileges, and injustices, each with its own malice and disdain for a God who loves us so much. No wonder the sacred heart of Jesus broke, no wonder his sacred blood burst forth from his veins!

And during this painful hour, Jesus seems to be saying: O my children, is this how you repay my love? O, if I could see you grateful, I would gladly be going to my death for you. But to see, even after my sufferings and death, still so many sins; to see, after my sacrifice of love, still so much ingratitude—this is what causes my precious blood to exude from my body as sweat!

At this juncture, Saint Matthew records that Jesus, feeling the heavy burden of our sins, fell to the ground: "And going a little farther, he threw himself on the ground and prayed" (Mt 26:39). It was as though he was ashamed to lift his eyes up to heaven. For a long time he lay there, face to the ground, praying.

PRAYER

O my Jesus, let me join you in prayer. In the garden of Gethsemane you asked the Father to have mercy on me, offering yourself to die for my sins. How can I not, then, surrender myself to such great love? How can I love anyone or anything more than you, my sweet Lord? Help me feel your sorrow, your pain. And by the merits of your agony in the garden, help me to deplore my past sins, and never sin again.

Mary, my hope, pray to Jesus for me. Amen.

TUESDAY
※

Jesus Is Made Prisoner and Led Away to Be Condemned

Judas, the traitor, now arrives at the garden. He immediately betrays his Master with a kiss. The soldiers, and those who accompanied them, take hold of Jesus and tie him up securely, as though he were a criminal. As Saint John tells it: "So the soldiers, their officer, and the Jewish police arrested Jesus and bound him" (Jn 18:12).

What is happening here? God is bound? How can this be? Who is arresting him? Who is tying him up? In fact, it was his own creatures! Angels of God, what have you to say about this?

Saint Bernard laments: "O King of kings, how is it that you are in chains?" Chains belong on criminals, or slaves, not on the King of kings, the Saint of saints. And even if men do dare to bind you, how is it that you do not burst your bonds and set yourself free? Ah, I know that it is not these ropes and chains which bind you; it is your love for us which makes you our captive, and condemns you to death.

Saint Bonaventure says: "Look how Jesus is maltreated! They drag him, they push him, they bind him, they strike him. Look at Jesus; he is like a gentle lamb being led to the sacrifice. Where are his disciples? Why do they not try to rescue him? Why do they not at least go along to defend him before the judges? But, as the Scriptures say, they abandoned him: "All of them deserted him and fled" (Mk 14:50).

O my abandoned Jesus, since that night in the garden, how many more people have also forsaken you? How many people, after consecrating themselves to follow you, after receiving so many special graces from you, have abandoned you because of some vile passion, or out of human respect, or for some profane pleasure! Unhappy me, that I have been one of these ungrateful ones! My Jesus, pardon me, for I wish nevermore to leave you. Amen.

Next, Jesus was brought before Caiaphas, the high priest, who questioned him about his disciples and his doctrine. Jesus patiently replied that he had always spoken not in private but publicly, and that he had preached daily in the temple. Even the bystanders could testify to this. Yet, this gentle response of Jesus prompted one of the servants of the high priest standing nearby to strike him a hard blow on the face, saying: "Is that how you answer the high priest?" (Jn 18:22).

Surely we may ask: how did such a simple response from Jesus provoke so great an insult before so many other people, and before even the high priest, who did not even reprimand his servant? What we have here is one more insult which Jesus suffered to make up for the many acts of imprudence we have committed in our own life.

The sad story continues. The high priest then asks Jesus an important question: "Are you the Messiah, the Son of the Blessed One?" (Mk 14:61). Jesus, out of respect for the Father's name, responded clearly: "I am" (Mk 14:62). Caiaphas then rent his garments and said that Jesus had blasphemed. He asked those present for a decision about what to do with Jesus. Of course, all condemned him, saying: "He deserves death" (Mt 26:66).

When this happened, a horrible scene took place. As Matthew tells us: "Then they spat in his face and struck him; and some slapped him, saying, 'Prophesy to us, you Messiah! Who is it that struck you?'" (Mt 26:67–68). They continued to insult and torment Jesus in this way all throughout the night.

Ah, my dear Jesus, these fiends strike you, buffet you, spit in your face, and you remain silent. Your are indeed "like a lamb that is led to the slaughter, and like a sheep that before its shearers is silent" (Isa 53:7). But if these, your enemies, do not know you, I know you, and I profess that you are my God and Savior. And now I understand that whatever sufferings you are to endure, it is all out of love for me. I thank you, my Jesus, and from now on I want to love you with all my heart. Amen.

When morning finally arrived, they led Jesus to Pilate, to have him condemned to death. At first, Pilate declared him innocent. However, as Saint Luke tells the story, when Pilate heard that Jesus was from Galilee, he wanted to get rid of Jesus, so he sent him to King Herod, who was then ruler over that area (see Lk 23:6–7). Herod had many foolish questions for Jesus, but he would answer none of them. Because of this, Herod had Jesus clothed in a white robe, the garb of a madman, and returned him to Pilate.

PRAYER

O my Jesus, you are eternal Wisdom, yet you are treated as a fool! And I, too, have sometimes rejected you! Do not punish me, as you did Herod, by depriving me of your voice or your inspirations. Herod did not recognize you for who you are; I acknowledge you as my God and Savior. Herod was not sorry for having offended you; I repent with all my heart for having done so. Tell me now what you would want of me, and by your grace, I will do your will.

Mary, my hope, pray to Jesus for me. Amen.

WEDNESDAY
☙

JESUS IS SCOURGED

The crowds continued to demand that Jesus be put to death, so with a kind of reverse logic, and in an attempt to pacify them, Pontius Pilate declared Jesus to be innocent, but then condemned him to be scourged. Saint Luke tells how this happened: "Pilate then called together the chief priests, the leaders, and the people, and said to them, 'You brought me this man as one who was perverting the people; and here I have examined him in your presence and have not found this man guilty of any of your charges against him…. Indeed, he has done nothing to deserve death. I will therefore have him flogged and release him" (Lk 23:13–16).

If Pilate thought that he would quiet Jesus' enemies in this manner, his contriving turned out to be more harmful to our Savior. Jesus' enemies insisted that the soldiers—some say they were even bribed to be excessively brutal—should beat Jesus to such a degree that he would die from this torment alone.

It was revealed to Saint Bridget that Jesus voluntarily took off his outer clothing for the scourging and embraced the pillar of stone used as the central site for this horrible punishment. The soldiers flogging Jesus were relentless. One struck him around his head and face, another his shoulders and back, another his thighs and other parts of his body. Picture his sacred blood flowing from countless wounds. See the scourgers, themselves covered with blood, their whips made crimson by the blood flowing from the wounds they were inflicting upon Jesus.

The scourging was incredibly torturous for Jesus: for one reason, there were dozens of soldiers involved in the process. Some of the saints, for example, Saint Mary Magdalene of Pazzi and Saint Bridget, have had revelations of the torments Jesus suffered. These revelations are so lurid and gruesome that they are almost unbelievable. After the scourging, Jesus was so badly beaten and bloodied that Pontius Pilate sought to extract some compassion from the mob by bringing Jesus before them, and proclaiming: "Ecce homo"—"Here is the man!" (Jn 19:5). But even that did not satisfy the cruel mob. They demanded more; they would be satisfied with nothing less than death.

Truly, as the prophet Isaiah had long ago predicted: "He was wounded for our transgressions, crushed for our iniquities" (Isa 53:5). This was the penalty which Jesus was willing to pay for our sins, especially our sins of impurity. His body was almost torn apart so that it truly became all sores and bruises. According to the holy visionaries, the very bones of his sides were laid bare: "He has borne our infirmities and carried our diseases; …struck down by God, and afflicted" (Isa 53:4).

PRAYER

O my Jesus, we are the ones who have offended God and you are the one who paid the penalty. May your divine charity be forever blessed! What would have been my lot, my Jesus, if you had not made satisfaction for me! I wish now that I had never offended God, my loving Father, and you, my loving Savior. But now I am truly sorry, and I hope for pardon. I hope that you have already pardoned me, and that in your goodness you already love me. Ah, my dear Redeemer, bind me ever more closely to yourself; never let me be separated from you again. Make me love you and then do with me as you will.

Mary, my hope, pray to Jesus for me. Amen.

THURSDAY

THE CROWNING WITH THORNS

The barbarian Roman soldiers, not content with having mangled the sacred body of Jesus by the cruel scourging, now began to mock our saving Lord by treating him as a false king. They threw a ragged scarlet robe over him to simulate a royal mantle and put a reed in his hand to serve as a scepter. Then they wove a crown out of thorns for his head, not only to ridicule him, but also to hurt him further, for they used the reed to pound the thorns deep into his holy head.

Saint Peter Damian wrote that the thorns pierced far into Jesus' head, penetrating even to the brain. And it was revealed to Saint Bridget that the crown of thorns caused his precious blood to flow to such an extent that it filled his eyes, and covered his face and his beard. Also, it must be said that the thorns inflicted the deepest and most prolonged pain to Jesus, a pain that was renewed every time he moved his head, a pain that continued until, at last, he bowed his head in death.

According to Saint Matthew (see Mt 27:27), the crowning with thorns took place in the governor's headquarters, with the whole cohort of soldiers plus the inevitable crowd of onlookers taking part. He tells how the soldiers, in their mockery of Jesus, also knelt before him, slapped him, spat upon him, and in derision, saluted him with the words: "Hail, King of the Jews!" (Mt 27:29).

O my Lord, you are indeed the king of heaven, but to what have you been reduced here on earth!

If a stranger had chanced that hour to pass by this disgraceful scene and seen this man thus disfigured, covered with purple rags, a thin reed scepter in his hand and a crown of thorns upon his head, the man being further derided and abused by a frenzied mob, what would he have thought, other than that this man must have been the most wicked and criminal person in the whole world! Behold how the Son of God became the mockery of Jerusalem!

PRAYER

O my Jesus, if I look at your body, I see nothing but wounds and blood. And if I look into your heart, I see only anguish and bitterness, which have made you suffer the agony of death. Who but a God could ever have humbled himself to suffer so much for his creatures—creatures who are still beloved because you are still God. Your wounds are indeed unquestionable signs of the love you bear us.

O, would that I could have seen you on that day when you were such a spectacle of reproach to all Jerusalem! Surely, then, I would have been overcome with love for you. Even so, now I wish to love you above all things, and I am ready to suffer and die in order to please you and you alone. Accept the sacrifice which I, a repentant sinner, offer you with all my heart.

Mary, my hope, continue to pray for me. Amen.

FRIDAY

✖

JESUS IS CONDEMNED TO DIE AND CARRY HIS CROSS TO CALVARY

Finally, Pontius Pilate, fearful of losing favor with Caesar, the emperor of Rome, condemned Jesus to die on the cross. He sentenced him to this horrible punishment and death, even though during the course of the trial, he had repeatedly declared him innocent.

Saint Bernard comments on this unjust judgment: "O my innocent Jesus, what crime have you committed that you should be condemned to die?" And then the saint himself replies: "I understand your crime; it is that you have loved us too much. This, rather than Pilate, condemns you."

And then the unjust sentence is read. Jesus hears it, accepts it, and submits to the will of the heavenly Father. As Saint Paul puts it: "He humbled himself and became obedient to the point of death—even death on a cross" (Phil 2:8).

After the sentence was read, the soldiers and the mob, in their fury, drag Jesus off to crucify him. He is again clothed in his own garments, the cross is brought for him to carry up Calvary's steep ascent. Jesus embraces and kisses his cross. It is as though he has been waiting thirty-three years to carry it to the site of his death, waiting his entire life to show his love for us.

Then, the King of heaven, heavily laden with his own cross, goes forth from the tribunal, accompanied by two thieves, who had also been condemned. Saint John describes the scene: "And carrying the cross by himself, he went out to what is called The

Place of the Skull, which in Hebrew is called Golgotha" (Jn 19:17). And, we may be sure, the angels of paradise went along, to accompany him in this way of death.

My soul, do you see your Lord, going to die for you? Look at him as he goes along the road, his head bowed down, his knees weakened, his body torn with wounds and dripping with his precious blood, a crown of thorns upon his head, and the heavy cross on his shoulders. Look at him walking with such difficulty that, at every step, he seems ready to die on the way. Ask him: Where, Lamb of God, are you going? Hear his answer: I go to die for you!

PRAYER

O my Jesus, I have been so forgetful of your love. But now I repent of all the wrongs I have done to you, and I ask forgiveness. Remind me always of the love which you have borne for me, and the patience you have shown me. Help me now to be faithful to you until my own death.

Mary my Mother and Queen, pray to Jesus for me. Amen.

SATURDAY

❧

THE CRUCIFIXION AND DEATH OF JESUS

We are now on Calvary's heights, which has become a theater of divine love, where a God dies for us in a sea of sorrow!

When Jesus arrived at Calvary, the soldiers stripped him of his garments, unmindful of his shame, as well as the pain caused when his torn flesh adhered to his clothing. They then flung him onto the cross and nailed him to it. This unwieldy instrument of death is raised, with Jesus hanging upon it supported only by nails that are driven through his hands and feet. Thus, he can find neither room nor rest, only the most bitter pain, for whichever way he leans, the torture increases.

On the cross, there is a sign which reads: "Jesus of Nazareth, the King of the Jews." But with the exception of this title of derision and scorn, what is there to show that Jesus is indeed a king? Ah, perhaps this throne of pain, these hands and feet pierced with nails, a head crowned with thorns, this torn and mutilated flesh, all these things make him known as a king; but a king of love!

O my Jesus, I thank you and I love you!

As he hangs on the cross, Jesus has few, if any, people to console him. Of all those standing beneath the cross, there are those who insult him, and others who mock him: "You who would destroy the temple and build it in three days, save yourself! If you are the Son of God, come down from the cross" (Mt 27:40). Still others said: "He saved others; he cannot save himself" (Mt 27:42).

Scripture tells us that even one of those criminals who was condemned to die with him had no compassion: "One of the criminals who were hanged there kept deriding him and saying, 'Are you not the Messiah? Save yourself and us!'" (Lk 23:39).

In truth, Mary, his holy Mother, was there beneath the cross, but this was of no consolation to Jesus, for the sight of her, standing there in such consummate sorrow and pain, made him feel even more devastated.

To whom could he turn? His heavenly Father? Yes, but the Father, seeing Jesus laden with all the unnumbered sins of humankind, for which he was making satisfaction, would have said to the Son: I cannot console you. Even I must abandon you, and let you die without comfort or consolation. And then Jesus uttered his heartbreaking cry: "My God, my God, why have you forsaken me?" (Mt 27:46).

With that, Jesus entered into the last moments of his earthly life. Only one more "word" needs to be spoken. Saint John describes the final moment: "When Jesus had received the wine, he said, 'It is finished.' Then he bowed his head and gave up his spirit" (Jn 19:30). It is as if he said to all of us: "O my creatures, all has been completed and done for your redemption. Now you must love me, for there is nothing more I can do to make you love me."

See what has happened to him on the cross! His eyes have grown dim, his face pale, his heart is barely beating, his sacred body has lost all signs of life, his soul is ready to burst into eternity. Then, let us also see what is happening all around him: the heavens are darkened, the earth trembles and quakes, tombs are opening, all nature mourns now that the creator of the world is about to die.

PRAYER

O my dead Savior, in spirit I draw near to your cross and embrace your feet, and I remember that you are dead only because of the love you have borne for me. Help me to understand, if only a little bit, how great your love must have been that a God should die for me. Now may I, in turn, from this day forward, love none other than you. By the merits of your death, make me die to all creatures and to every thing that would separate me from you in any way. May I love you alone for you alone are worthy of my love.

Hail Jesus, my love, and Mary, my hope. Amen.

Saint Alphonsus Liguori's Way of the Cross

Preparatory Prayer

My Lord Jesus Christ, you have made this journey to die for me with unspeakable love, and I have again and again ungratefully abandoned you. But now I love you with all my heart, and because I love you, I am sorry for having sinned. Pardon me, my God, and allow me to go with you on this journey. You accepted your cross because of your great love for me; I desire, my beloved Redeemer, to die for love of you. My Jesus, I will live and die always united to you.

FIRST STATION:
JESUS IS CONDEMNED TO DEATH

V. We adore you, O Christ, and we praise you.

R. Because by your holy cross you have redeemed the world.

Consider that Jesus, after having been scourged and crowned with thorns, was unjustly condemned by Pilate to die on the cross.

My Jesus, it was not Pilate, no, it was my sins that condemned you to die. I ask you, by the merits of this sorrowful journey, to assist my soul in its journey toward eternity. I love you more than myself. I repent with my whole heart of having offended you. Never permit me to separate myself from you again. Grant that I may love you always; and then do with me what you will.

Conclude this station with an Our Father, a Hail Mary, and a Glory Be.

SECOND STATION:
JESUS IS MADE TO BEAR HIS CROSS

V. We adore you, O Christ, and we praise you.

R. Because by your holy cross you have redeemed the world.

Consider that Jesus, in making this journey with the cross on his shoulders, thought of us, and offered for us to his Father the death that he was about to undergo.

My beloved Jesus, I embrace all the tribulations that you have destined for me until my death. I ask you, by the merits of the pain you did suffer in carrying your cross, to give me the necessary help to carry my cross with perfect patience and resignation. I love you, Jesus. I repent for having offended you. Grant that I may love you always, and then do with me what you will.

Conclude this station with an Our Father, a Hail Mary, and a Glory Be.

THIRD STATION: JESUS FALLS THE FIRST TIME

V. We adore you, O Christ, and we praise you.

R. Because by your holy cross you have redeemed the world.

Consider this first fall of Jesus under his cross. His flesh was torn by the scourges, his head crowned with thorns, and he had lost a great quantity of blood. He was so weakened that he could scarcely walk, and yet he had to carry this great load upon his shoulders. The soldiers struck him rudely, and thus he fell several times in his journey.

My beloved Jesus, it is not the weight of the cross, but of my sins that have made you suffer so much pain. Oh, by the merits of this first fall, deliver me from the misfortune of falling into mortal sin. I love you, O my Jesus, with my whole heart. I repent of having offended you. Never permit me to offend you again. Grant that I may love you always; and then do with me what you will.

Conclude this station with an Our Father, a Hail Mary, and a Glory Be.

FOURTH STATION:
JESUS MEETS HIS MOTHER

V. We adore you, O Christ, and we praise you.

R. Because by your holy cross you have redeemed the world.

Consider the meeting of the Son and the Mother, which took place on this journey. Jesus and Mary looked at each other, and their looks became as so many arrows to wound those hearts that loved each other so tenderly.

Most loving Jesus, by the sorrow you experienced in this meeting, grant me the grace of a truly devoted love for your most holy mother. And you, my Queen, who was overwhelmed with sorrow, obtain for me by your intercession a continual and tender remembrance of the passion of your son. I love you, Jesus; I repent of ever having offended you. Never permit me to offend you again. Grant that I may love you, and then do with me what you will.

Conclude this station with an Our Father, a Hail Mary, and a Glory Be.

FIFTH STATION:
SIMON HELPS JESUS TO CARRY HIS CROSS

V. We adore you, O Christ, and we praise you.

R. Because by your holy cross you have redeemed the world.

Consider that the Jews, seeing that at each step Jesus was on the point of expiring, and fearing that he would die on the way, when they wished him to die the ignominious death of the cross, constrained Simon the Cyrenian to carry the cross behind our Lord.

My sweet Jesus, I will not refuse the cross as Simon the Cyrenian did. I accept it, I embrace it. I accept in particular the death that you have destined for me, with all the pains that may accompany it. I unite it to your death, I offer it to you. You have died for love of me. I will die for love of you. Help me by your grace. I love you, Jesus; I repent of having offended you. Never permit me to offend you again. Grant that I may love you; and then do with me what you will.

Conclude this station with an Our Father, a Hail Mary, and a Glory Be.

Sixth Station:
Veronica Wipes the Face of Jesus

V. We adore you, O Christ, and we praise you.

R. Because by your holy cross you have redeemed the world.

Consider that the holy woman named Veronica, seeing Jesus so afflicted, and his face bathed in sweat and blood, presented him with a towel, with which he wiped his face, leaving on it the impression of his holy countenance.

My beloved Jesus, your face was beautiful before, but in this journey it has lost all its beauty, and wounds and blood have disfigured it. My soul was also once beautiful, when it received your grace in baptism; but I have disfigured it since by my sins. You alone, my Redeemer, can restore it to its former beauty. Do this by your passion, and then do with me what you will.

Conclude this station with an Our Father, a Hail Mary, and a Glory Be.

Seventh Station:
Jesus Falls the Second Time

V. We adore you, O Christ, and we praise you.

R. Because by your holy cross you have redeemed the world.

Consider the second fall of Jesus under the cross—a fall which renews the pain of all the wounds of the head and members of our afflicted Lord.

My most gentle Jesus, how many times have you pardoned

me, and how many times have I fallen again, and begun again to offend you. By the merits of this new fall, give me the necessary helps to persevere in your grace until death. Grant that in all temptations that assail me I may always commend myself to you. I love you, Jesus, with my whole heart. I repent of having offended you. Never permit me to offend you again. Grant that I may love you always; and then do with me what you will.

Conclude this station with an Our Father, a Hail Mary, and a Glory Be.

EIGHTH STATION:
JESUS SPEAKS TO THE DAUGHTERS OF JERUSALEM

V. We adore you, O Christ, and we praise you.

R. Because by your holy cross you have redeemed the world.

Consider that those women wept with compassion at seeing Jesus in so pitiable a state, streaming with blood, as he walked along. But Jesus said to them, "Weep not for me, but for your children."

My Jesus, laden with sorrows, I weep for the sins I have committed against you, because of the pains which they have deserved, and still more because of the displeasure which they have caused you, who has loved me so much. It is your love, more than the fear of hell, which causes me to weep for my sins. My Jesus, I love you more than myself. I repent of having offended you. Never permit me to offend you again. Grant that I may love you always; and then do with me as you will.

Conclude this station with an Our Father, a Hail Mary, and a Glory Be.

NINTH STATION:
JESUS FALLS THE THIRD TIME

V. We adore you, O Christ, and we praise you.
R. Because by your holy cross you have redeemed the world.

Consider the third fall of Jesus Christ. His weakness was extreme, and the cruelty of his executioners excessive, who tried to hasten his steps when he had scarcely strength to move.

Oh, my outraged Jesus, by the merits of the weakness that you suffered in going to Calvary, give me strength sufficient to conquer all human respect and all my wicked passions, which have led me to despise your friendship. I love you, Jesus, with my whole heart; I repent of having offended me. Never permit me to offend you again. Grant that I may love you always; and then do with me what you will.

Conclude this station with an Our Father, a Hail Mary, and a Glory Be.

TENTH STATION:
JESUS IS STRIPPED OF HIS GARMENTS

V. We adore you, O Christ, and we praise you.

R. Because by your holy cross you have redeemed the world.

Consider the violence with which the executioners stripped Jesus. His inner garments adhered to his torn flesh, and they dragged them off so roughly the skin came with them. I offer my compassion to you, my Savior, who are so cruelly treated.

My innocent Jesus, by the merits of the torment that you have felt, help me to strip myself of all affection toward things of the earth, in order that I may place all my love in you, who are so worthy of my love. I love you, O Jesus, with my whole heart; I repent of having offended you. Never permit me to offend you again. Grant that I may love you always; and then do with me what you will.

Conclude this station with an Our Father, a Hail Mary, and a Glory Be.

ELEVENTH STATION:
JESUS IS NAILED TO THE CROSS

V. We adore you, O Christ, and we praise you.

R. Because by your holy cross you have redeemed the world.

Consider that Jesus, after being thrown on the cross, extended his hands, and offered to his Eternal Father the sacrifice of his life for our salvation. These barbarians fastened him with nails; and then, raising the cross, left him to die with anguish on this infamous gibbet.

My Jesus, loaded with contempt, nail my heart to your feet, that it may ever remain there to love you, and never quit you again. I love you more than myself; I repent of having offended you. Never permit me to offend you again. Grant that I may love you always; and then do with me what you will.

Conclude this station with an Our Father, a Hail Mary, and a Glory Be.

TWELFTH STATION:
JESUS DIES ON THE CROSS

V. We adore you, O Christ, and we praise you.

R. Because by your holy cross you have redeemed the world.

Consider that Jesus, after three hours of agony on the cross, consumed at length with anguish, abandons himself to the weight of his body, bows his head, and dies.

O my dying Jesus, I kiss the cross on which you died for love of me. I have merited by my sins to die a miserable death; but your death is my hope. By the merits of your death, give me the grace to die, embracing your cross and burning with love for you. I commit my soul into your hands. I repent of ever having offended you. Permit me never to offend you again. Grant that I may love you always; and then do with me as you will.

Conclude this station with an Our Father, a Hail Mary, and a Glory Be.

THIRTEENTH STATION: JESUS IS TAKEN DOWN FROM THE CROSS

V. We adore you, O Christ, and we praise you.

R. Because by your holy cross you have redeemed the world.

Consider that our Lord having died, two of his disciples, Joseph and Nicodemus, took him down from the cross, and placed him in the arms of his afflicted mother, who received him with unimaginable tenderness and pressed him to her heart.

O Mother of sorrow, for the love of this son, accept me for your servant, and pray to him for me. And you, my Redeemer, since you have died for me, permit me to love you; for I wish only you, and nothing more. I love you, my Jesus, and I repent of ever having offended you. Never permit me to offend you again. Grant that I may love you always; and then do with me what you will.

Conclude this station with an Our Father, a Hail Mary, and a Glory Be.

FOURTEENTH STATION:
JESUS IS PLACED IN THE SEPULCHER

V. We adore you, O Christ, and we praise you.

R. Because by your holy cross you have redeemed the world.

Consider that the disciples carried the body of Jesus to bury it, accompanied by his holy mother, who arranged it in the tomb with her own hands. They then closed the tomb and all withdrew.

My buried Jesus, I kiss the stone that encloses you. But you rose again on the third day. I beseech you, by your resurrection, make me rise glorious with you at the last day, to be always united with you in heaven, to praise you and love you forever. I love you, and I repent of ever having offended you. Permit me never to offend you again. Grant that I may love you; and then do with me as you will.

Conclude this last station with an Our Father, a Hail Mary, and a Glory Be.